3

NEVER TOO OLD TO

NEVER TOO OLD TO

Rock & Roll

LIFE AFTER 50 —
THE BEST YEARS YET

Thomas L. Hardin

with Gail Fink

Canterbury Publishing  Zionsville, Indiana

NEVER TOO OLD TO ROCK & ROLL

This publication contains the opinions and ideas of its author. It is intended to provide helpful and informative material on the subjects covered. It is sold with the understanding that neither the author nor the publisher is engaged in rendering medical, nutritional, or any other kind of personal or professional service. The advice and strategies contained herein may not be suitable for your situation. Consult your medical, nutritional, or other competent professional before adopting any of the suggestions in this book or drawing inferences from them.

The financial section of this book is intended as a thought-provoking exploration of the investment horizon resulting from the author's observation in the hope that you'll continue the question-asking process. The prices, quotes, and statistics used in preparing this material were obtained from sources that we believe to be reliable, but we cannot guarantee their accuracy or completeness. No guarantees can be issued as to future performance in any of the areas discussed; nor is this an offer or solicitation with respect to the purchase or sale of any security. Before making any investment decision, obtain the advice of a qualified investment professional.

Canterbury Publishing Group, LLC
23 East Cedar Street
Zionsville, IN 46077

Attention Organizations and Corporations

Special discounts on large quantities of Canterbury Publishing books are available to corporations, professional associations, and other organizations. For details, please contact Canterbury Publishing at 800.340.0234.

Special thanks to Authors of Unity

Printed in the United States

ISBN 0-9761374-0-2
Library of Congress Control Number: 2004112834

To my wife, Kim—

may we rock and roll forever!

CONTENTS

ACKNOWLEDGMENTS

First, I would like to thank my wife, Kim, for her unwavering support and for being a sounding board for the three years it took to produce this book. Her constant encouragement and commonsense advice have been invaluable.

Next, I want to thank my collaborator and friend, Gail Fink. Gail's research skill, writing ability, and insight were the keys to making this book one of the best in its subject area.

Steve Moeller changed my life with his coaching. Three years ago, he suggested that I interview ideal role models in an effort to become an expert on life after 50. The result is this book. Steve has been an absolutely invaluable resource, a tremendous influence, and a generous contributor to this project. I couldn't have written this book without his wisdom and advice.

Thanks to Cheryl Kahn and Kim Dale for reviewing rough drafts, providing organizational assistance, keeping me on track, and being a never-ending source of encouragement and support.

I would like to thank Dr. Craig Overmyer for his mentoring in the area of personal life vision coaching and his contributions to this book. Craig is the best in his field of expertise.

Tom Miller and his team at Miller Brooks, Inc., coined the title, *Never Too Old to Rock and Roll,* and designed the cover. I cannot thank them enough for their rockin' and rollin' creativity.

Christian Gurgone and his team at Authors of Unity transformed the finished manuscript into the beautiful book you hold in your hands. Special thanks go to interior book designer Deborah Rutti and copywriter Susan Kendrick.

Thanks to Bennett Fisher and Jen Stacklin, who created the best Web site on the Internet, www.nevertooold.com.

Special thanks to Ron Robbins and Sid Corder, who both thought they were interviewees and found that they became sounding boards. I also appreciate all the listening, reviewing, and encouragement provided by my family over the past three years.

I extend my deep appreciation to the many professionals who made critical contributions: Sheva Carr; Joseph Farah; Fritz French; Richard Haid, PhD; Kimberly A. Hardin, RD; Todd Harris, MD; Bill Hartman, PT, CSCS; Brad Herndon, CMT, CFA; Frank Hoffman, JD; Mark Kershisnik, RPh; Norma Keywan, RN, NCTMB; G. Nick Kruskall, MS; Laura Kruskall, PhD, RD; William Martz; Reverend Sandra B. Michels; Steve Midkiff; William Nasser, MD; Dave Oeschger, PhD; Young Park, DO; Douglas H. Rapelje, FCCHSE; Laura Rubinstein; Teresa Tanoos of *Healthy Living with Teresa Tanoos;* Dick Wolfsie; and David Wong, MD. Thanks also to Pat McKeand and Joe Keesey, who worked with me on earlier versions of the text.

Throughout this project, I interviewed hundreds of amazing individuals about the issues they've faced as they journeyed toward their best years yet. I can honestly say I never conducted an interview without being astonished at the insights each person provided. I thank you all.

Last but not least, I'd like to thank my next-door neighbor, Jerry Klapper, who's ten years older than me and gives me constant feedback about what it's like to be old.

AUTHOR'S NOTE

In the chapters that follow, you'll meet some outstanding individuals. Their stories are not caricatures, nor are they compilations created by blending different people together. Each story is true and presented exactly as it was told to me. To protect their privacy, I omitted contributors' last names and used fictitious first names upon request.

FOREWORD

The future's not what it used to be. It seemed so simple for our depression-era parents and grandparents. For most of them, the future was automatically mapped out—go to school, get a job, raise a family, and then retire, hopefully with a pension and a Social Security check.

The pension my grandparents earned from working in a factory gave them the opportunity to retire. I treasure the memories of sitting with Grandpa Wilmer on his front porch. Usually with a pipe in his mouth and not too worried about anything but his garden, he'd wave at the neighbors as they drove by. Grandma Grace lovingly greeted the constant flow of grandchildren. She was usually cooking in the kitchen, with the aroma of fresh-baked cookies drawing us kids like bees to a hive. Having a place for the family to gather for Sunday dinner was my grandparents' main focus. For them, the future just happened. It didn't take much planning or forethought.

The future won't happen automatically for us. Too much has changed. Why, most of the kids growing up in today's global community, connected with the Internet and iPods, don't have memories of Sunday dinners at their grandparents' house. "We don't have time," is the common excuse.

Why not? Where are we going in our mad daily dash? Ultimately, we're headed to our graves, and we're writing our obituaries through the choices we make along the way. What's the rush? Let's slow down, cherish this book, and put into practice its powerful and urgent message: Life after 50 can be our best years yet—*if* we have the commitment, vision, and courage to create and follow our own maps for the future.

If you slow down enough to take in the wisdom and guidance in this book, you'll be amazed at how much attention you'll be able to put toward shaping your best possible future. You're on the greatest treasure hunt of your life, and this book is a map for the journey. Tom Hardin is a futurist who sees trends for today's aging population. He offers help as you face possibilities and perils unknown to previous generations.

Don't make the mistake of dashing through time, aimlessly letting the years just happen. The possibility of living longer and creating a purposeful life requires visioning and planning with intention. Read this book, have a spirit of adventure, and remember—you're never too old to rock and roll!

Dr. Craig Overmyer
Contributing author, *Dynamic Health* and
Success Is a Decision of the Mind

INTRODUCTION

Two unprecedented events are sweeping America—
10,000 people turn 50 *every day*, and we're living longer
than ever before. As the generation that once said "you
can't trust anyone over 30" rapidly approaches its 65th birthday,
advancements in technology, medicine, nutrition, and other key
areas are letting us feel younger and live to be older than any generation has in the past. In the next few years, everything we think
we know about middle age and beyond will change . . . but how?

Many so-called experts predict the aging baby boomers will
become an albatross around America's neck—overwhelming the
healthcare system, bankrupting Social Security, hoarding our
wealth, and retreating to retirement villages where we'll refuse to
support schools and social services with our taxes. This book
offers a radically different perspective: Life after 50 can be *our
best years yet!*

How can I make such a radical claim? As a personal wealth
manager and technical analyst, I'm a close observer of trends, and
a new longevity trend has already begun. As people are reaching
their mid to late 60s, a few innovative thinkers are taking a radically different approach to those years. So far, they're only a small
percentage, but they're continuing to work beyond the age when
they could realistically retire. They're using part of their savings to
turn hobbies into income producers, retrain for second careers, or
start businesses of their own. They're remaining active in their
companies and communities by heading up boards of directors
and providing valuable leadership based on their vast experience.
These bold pioneers are forging a path for baby boomers to follow.

The same thing happened in the 1950s and '60s, when a few
members of this older group led the countercultural revolution.
They were the real trailblazers in areas like civil rights, feminism,
voter reform—and rock and roll. When baby boomers embraced
their ideas, the revolution exploded.

That's one of the reasons I've coined a new term that combines this older group with the boomers who followed. I call people born between 1937 and 1957 the *rock and roll generation,* and I'm proud to be a member.

What makes people from our generation behave so differently from our parents and grandparents before us? Take a moment to consider the following:

The rock and roll generation is different from any other. Unlike the previous generation, whose memories of the Great Depression and World War II left them worried about the future and world events, rock and rollers have always been creative, optimistic, unafraid of change, and young at heart. We believe the best is yet to come.

We have a different attitude, and attitude is everything. We're the rock and roll generation—always have been, always will be. When we're 100 years old, we'll still be the rock and roll generation. We'll never consider ourselves "seniors," no matter how old we get.

We're living a lifestyle we love and we don't want it to end. Rather than retiring to inactivity, we feel like kids out of high school: As we reach the end of one career, we face a number of options. Many opportunities are ours for the taking, and with a little planning, we'll have the wisdom, insight, intuition, and money to make our dreams come true.

Rock and rollers are a generation of revolution and new ideas. We've changed everything we've ever cared about, from voting rights to civil rights, from how we raise our kids to how we relate in the workplace. Now we care about aging, and we're going to do it like it's never been done before.

Life after 50 can be our best years yet, but a life of total abundance won't happen automatically. To enjoy healthy longevity, we'll have to create the possibility for it to occur. We'll need to develop the physical, mental, spiritual, emotional—and yes, financial—readiness to face what many consider the retirement years. Since we're likely to live longer than we may have imagined, we may need or want to continue working beyond age 65. To do that, we'll need to be in good shape physically, financially, mentally, and emotionally. That's what this book is all about.

In the chapters that follow, I'll share with you my seven keys for personal wealth management and show you how you can create total abundance by applying them to critical areas of life. Using the simple steps outlined in this book, you'll soon see that managing your wealth means creating more abundance *in all areas of life*—not just financially, but in terms of your health, happiness, wisdom, and experience. You'll discover . . .

- The powerful impact of a compelling vision of your future
- How to unleash the strength and vitality to do the things you love, for as long as you want
- How to adjust your career to meet your changing personal and financial needs in life after 50
- Proven portfolio and wealth management strategies for creating lifelong financial freedom
- The untapped secrets to a long, healthy life

The first and perhaps most important key is taking time to envision a compelling future. By defining your vision for the coming years, then designing a plan to achieve it, you can reap a rich harvest—the attainment and celebration of that vision.

The rock and roll generation was the first group to embrace the concepts of exercise, good nutrition, and a healthy lifestyle. Now it's time to go one step further—to achieve outstanding physical well-being by applying the seven keys to those areas of life. Taking advantage of all the opportunities available to you—like continuing to work or starting a new career, traveling, mentoring the younger generation, and enjoying the things you're passionate about—will be much more fun and enjoyable if you're in the best physical condition you can possibly achieve. You'll also need strong relationships, a good mental attitude, and a healthy emotional and spiritual foundation.

Few things in life are more stressful than not having enough money. You can probably think back to a time when you didn't have an adequate amount and remember how all-consuming and miserable it felt. Or maybe you remember your parents' or grandparents' descriptions of living through the Great Depression. Being scarcity thinkers, they preached principles like, "Clean your plate," and "Money doesn't grow on trees."

Because of their strong message about working hard today and saving for the future, you probably learned from the older generation that saving meant sacrifice. You may even have forgone some current consumption in exchange for a vague reward in the years ahead. However, as those years draw ever closer, it's apparent that many people in our generation haven't saved enough. If you're one of them, it's time to focus on your finances and develop new ways to become financially independent. It's time to get away from scarcity thinking and adopt a new attitude of abundance thinking. In other words, it's time to get serious about managing your money so you can use it as a tool to achieve total wealth and abundance in all areas of life.

This book offers a new approach to finances called *personal wealth management*. You'll discover the kind of conversation you should be having with your financial advisor, revolving more around connecting your money to your quality of life. You'll also learn how important it is to take a renewed interest in your assets and get a good background about how they should be managed so they can supplement and enhance your life, both now and in the future.

Finally, we'll look at the exciting possibilities that can result from applying the seven keys to life's critical areas. What will the future hold for the rock and roll generation? What can you look forward to in life after 50, your best years yet?

You have a simple choice: You can define your future life or let others define it for you. I for one, intend to be a definer, not a definee. I've already begun envisioning my future, and so can you.

If you believe that getting older means struggling to live within your means, falling apart at the seams, and giving up on your dreams, this is not the book for you. But if the future I've described appeals to you—if you want to make life after 50 your *best* years yet and if you're open to the possibility that it really can happen— then get ready to rock and roll!

By the way, you don't have to be over 50 to benefit from this book. If you want to be sure you'll have the time, energy, and money to live the way you want and contribute to your family and community in meaningful ways, it's never too soon to start planning your future. If you're open-minded, curious, and willing to consider new ideas, I invite you to use this book as a catalyst for developing and achieving the future you desire.

That future can start now, today. Are you ready? Then turn the page and join me, because it's never too late to live your dreams, and you're never too old to rock and roll.

◆ ◆ ◆

Chapter 1

GET READY
FOR A REVOLUTION

W hat an exciting time to be alive! As the largest generation in America's history rapidly approaches retirement age, people are living longer than ever before. A thousand years ago, the average life expectancy was 25 years. A hundred years ago, it was 47. Today the average life expectancy is 75, and centenarians are the fastest-growing segment of our population—their numbers have tripled in the last two decades.

Ken Dychtwald, a noted gerontologist and the author of *Age Wave*, says we're in a longevity revolution. He envisions scientific breakthroughs in the near future that will eliminate osteoporosis, allow men to regrow hair, reverse or prohibit prostate enlargement, and rejuvenate the skin. He expects significant advancements in the study of autoimmune diseases such as arthritis and AIDS. For the first time in human evolution, we may be able to alter the way we age. By the year 2050, Dychtwald believes the average life expectancy may reach age 90. Think about that for a minute. If he's correct and if you're 50 years old today, there's a very good chance you'll live to be 90 or older.

You'd think this increased longevity would be a wonderful thing, but it raises some serious questions. If we live to be that old, will we have enough money to be financially independent for the rest of our lives? Will millions of baby boomers leave the workforce at age 65 and expect Social Security to support them for 20, 30, or

40 more years? Will our economy recover from the bear market and corporate scandals, or did those events cause irreparable damage to our pension and 401(k) plans? What happens to succeeding generations if Social Security goes bust, as many experts predict it will? Will our children have to shoulder the burden and support not just themselves, but an aging population as well? Can anything be done to ensure the future?

Finances aren't the only area of concern. Can we stay healthy and vibrant as we age? What's our purpose in life when we're older? Will we have the freedom to do what we want?

We hear these questions from economic analysts and the popular media. They expect the aging population to become a tremendous burden, requiring more care and attention than succeeding generations can possibly provide. They expect us to overwhelm the healthcare system and become a drain on society. Well, I have a few projections of my own. Unlike those doom-and-gloom predictors of disaster, I believe life after 50 can be our best years yet.

Yes, you read that correctly. I said *our best years yet.* Like many people, I used to believe that getting older meant getting worse. A few short years ago, I changed my opinion.

A Golf Course Epiphany

"Nothing is so intolerable to man as being fully at rest, without a passion, without business, without entertainment, without care."
—Blaise Pascal, 17th-century philosopher

Playing golf one day, I found myself thinking about my life. I used to do that quite a bit—visioning about the future was one of my strengths. For some reason, though, over the preceding years I'd spent less time focusing on what was next. This day was different. Maybe it was just one of those days, or maybe it happened because I wasn't playing that well, which generally depresses me anyway. Maybe it was brought on by my impending 50th birthday just a year or so away. At any rate, I started thinking about how great things were. I had a wonderful marriage, had just built my dream house, and was doing well in my career as a portfolio manager with a major investment firm. Business was good, the markets were up—yet I felt like something was missing. I found myself asking, *Is this it?*

My thoughts turned to the things I hadn't accomplished in life, and I wondered whether it was too late now. Were my best years already behind me? Could I still accomplish the things I'd always thought I would? Had I lived up to my potential, or had I failed to do so? I thought back to my 40th birthday, when family and friends regaled me with bunches of black balloons, gag gifts wrapped in little black coffins, and cards proclaiming me "over the hill." If the world thinks 40 is over the hill, what does it say about people in their 50s?

I remember going home and telling my wife, "I think I'll just grow the business another 50 percent, and then I'll slow down and focus on golf." I hoped that decision would make me feel better, but it only left me more depressed than ever.

The more I thought about my life, the less satisfied I felt. I realized I hadn't been learning or growing in my career. Attending corporate retreats, I'd find myself avoiding the workshops and heading for the golf course. I felt like I'd learned all my firm had to teach and those conferences were just a big waste of time. In fact, on one such occasion, my buddy and I devised a game we called "express golf." The object was to get up early, eat a quick breakfast with the group, then blow off the morning meetings, catch a van to the nearest golf course, play a quick round, and be back in time for lunch and the afternoon activities.

If anyone loves to learn, it's me. I've always focused on continuing education and pursuing all the designations that interested me. I honestly don't know of anyone who's earned more designations in more varied areas of the industry than I have. I'd spent more than three years earning my Chartered Market Technician designation, completing the requirements in 1997, but since that point, I'd felt kind of stagnant. I'd always enjoyed managing my clients' portfolios, but I wasn't being challenged in my current environment, and I certainly wasn't growing. After 25 years in the business, I couldn't see myself settling for the status quo, so I decided to reinvent myself.

About that time, baby boomers were growing more interested in strategizing about their futures, and financial planning was making a comeback. Deciding to revisit a field I'd once found intriguing, I began reading about the current direction of financial planning. That led me to explore some of the more interesting philosophies people had about money, and I stumbled across a book that resonated with me—*Effort-less Marketing for Financial Advisors*, by business coach Steve Moeller. His ideas were totally different from anything I'd heard in the industry before. He urged financial professionals to integrate their lives and their businesses by getting to know more about their clients on a personal level and focusing on the clients' values and goals in addition to the money management process. After reading his book, I called Steve and enrolled in his coaching program.

Steve Moeller literally changed my life. One of the first exercises we went through addressed my specific concern: not really knowing what was next for me. In the exercise, Steve instructed, "Pretend you can't do what you're doing anymore. What would you do instead?" For about half an hour, I struggled with that question. I came up with four one-word answers: golf, travel, read, and teach. While I'm passionate about each of those things, none seemed to be the solution I sought. I was already playing plenty of golf. I often found traveling more stressful than soothing or fun. I enjoyed reading, but everything I read was about business and information, and if I weren't in the business, what would I read? The same was true about teaching: If I couldn't be an investment manager, I wouldn't have anything to teach. I felt totally clueless. I simply couldn't conceive of a life without work, and I suddenly realized I didn't want to retire or even think about slowing down.

The rest is history. With Steve's help, I started looking at my business and my life in a whole new way. I found a new direction, I focused on the areas I was passionate about, and I delegated most other activities. A client of mine had recently sold his company and we'd worked together to develop a customized strategy for investing the proceeds. We focused on how his accumulated money could give him the freedom to pursue a whole new life. I really liked helping him through that process and realized I enjoyed working with people who were going through transitions. It didn't take long to go one step further and figure out that I wanted to work with people who were facing the same dilemma I'd faced—successful individuals who'd achieved a great deal in life and didn't want it to end just because they reached a certain age.

One day, I mentioned to Steve that I'd been working for some time on a book about investing. With his encouragement, I decided to broaden the topic. With his help, I also met Gail Fink, a freelance writer who became my collaborator on the project. Over the next three years, Gail and I did extensive research and seriously studied what life after 50 will be like. We read countless books on aging, longevity, and retirement, and interviewed hundreds of people who seemed happy and had made successful transitions from one stage of life to the next. As our enthusiasm for the subject grew, I left the company I'd been working with and started my own personal wealth management firm where my team and I focus on providing client-centered advice. We've developed cutting-edge tools and techniques to help our clients achieve total wealth and abundance in all their forms.

Today my vision for the future is so much broader than the one I came up with in Steve's seminar, and I'm so passionate about it that I'm pulled out of bed every morning with more energy and enthusiasm than I've ever felt before. Instead of slowing down and focusing on my golf game, I've set my sights on becoming an expert at helping people make life after 50 the best years yet. I can honestly tell you that I'm having more fun in my 50s than I did in my 40s—and that's saying something, because

I had more fun in my 40s than I did in my 30s, and more fun in my 30s than I did in my 20s. *And you can, too!* Rock and roll is an attitude, and we never have to lose it.

Yes, we'll face a number of transitions after age 50, but I believe we're up to the challenge. As you'll learn in the next few pages, we're part of an innovative generation whose leaders are already developing creative, nontraditional alternatives to life after 50 and the concept of retirement. Those bold pioneers are forging the path to something we can all enjoy—healthy longevity. Let's take a look at these leaders and what we can learn from their example.

The Changing Face of Aging

Looking for role models to emulate, we might be tempted to turn to our parents and grandparents. News anchor and author Tom Brokaw called this group "the Greatest Generation," and he was right. They overcame some real adversity. They spent their youth in the Great Depression, growing up in an era of scarcity and learning what it feels like when there's not enough to go around. (They call it a depression for a reason—it's depressing!) That awful period was followed by something even worse: World War II. Then came the atomic age, when people feared that someone might push a button at any moment and obliterate the entire planet.

I'd hate to think of what the world and society would look like today had it not been for the sacrifices of the Greatest Generation. Their experiences made the world a better place but left a lasting and important impression on them—and, as a result, on us, too.

HeadlightVision Ltd., a London-based research consultancy company, studied more than 40,000 people over age 45. They identified the core values and characteristic behavior of four separate groups, including the one we know as the Greatest Generation. HeadlightVision calls them "Stoic Seniors," and identifies them as people born between 1926 and 1935. Not surprisingly, this group tends to be cautious, conservative, and conscientious with a strong sense of family duty. They're usually thrifty, even when affluent, and they respect sacrifice. They "make do" and make the best of what they have. They pay their bills promptly and dislike surprises.

After living through a depression, a world war, and the dawning of the atomic age, it's no wonder they developed those traits and behaviors. They grew up believing that conditions were bad today and they could be even worse tomorrow. In general, this group wasn't too crazy about change, and they looked forward to a quiet, stable future.

I can understand how they came to feel that way. Back in April 1974, I lived in Louisville, Kentucky, when multiple tornadoes raged through the town. Houses were knocked down, the convention center roof was blown off, and the whole city looked as if it had been bombed. For the next year or so, every time we had a big storm, everyone in Louisville headed for their basements; that month of killer tornadoes had really left its mark. I can only imagine what it must have been like for the Greatest Generation after the years of adversity they endured. One horrendous event after another kept happening to those people, and for better or worse, it made them who they are today.

For many people in our parents' generation, growing up during the depression resulted in low expectations, conservative thinking, and an unwillingness to spend a lot of money. "Waste not, want not" became their mantra. Most of them were employed by just one company throughout their working years. Not surprisingly, the concept of retirement took root in that generation. Prior to the Great Depression, the majority of Americans did not believe government should care for the aged, disabled, or needy. After the depression, those attitudes changed. Many workers had learned firsthand that they could suffer from events over which they had no control, and they looked to the government for help and protection.

With the development of Social Security in 1935 and its expansion over the subsequent years, people began working 40,

50, or 60 hours a week. Working hard allayed their fears, but it resulted in an out-of-balance lifestyle. As a result, they looked forward to retiring to something completely opposite and equally out of balance—40 to 60 hours of "leisure time" each week, when many would go from overwork and overstress to a life of absolute boredom.

Growing up under drastically different circumstances, our generation embraced a different set of values and behaviors. HeadlightVision describes people born between 1936 and 1955 as liberal, socially tolerant individuals with a live-for-the-moment attitude. We're determined to stay young and redefine middle age, and we have a greater desire for balance between our work and our lives. Using our parents or grandparents as role models for aging simply won't work for us. We need a new paradigm about what those years can bring. Luckily for us, the answers lie within our midst, in the oldest segment of our own generation.

Birth Waves and Baby Booms

Much attention has been focused on the baby boomers, the generation born mostly as the offspring of American military personnel returning from World War II. According to the U.S. Census Bureau, baby boomers include everyone born from 1946 through 1964.

Because of my experience in the financial arena, I have a slightly different take on the term *baby boom.* To me, a boom is a period of explosive growth. In the stock market, it refers to the span of time between the bottom and the top of a market, or between the trough and the peak. A boom ends when the market begins to decline again. Although the Census Bureau extends the baby boom through 1964, I don't believe the declining years (after 1957) should be included.

If you look at 20th-century population growth (see the following figure), it's easy to see where the true boom occurred. It consisted of three clear-cut surges or waves: 1937 to 1945, 1945 to

The Real Baby Boom
1937–1957

1950, and 1950 to 1957. After 1957, the growth rate actually began to decline. The true boom in births occurred from 1937 to 1957, creating the group I call the *rock and roll generation.*

Now let's take a closer look at the significance of the three birth waves. In his book, *The Great Boom Ahead* (Hyperion, 1993), Harvard economist Harry S. Dent described the typical development cycle or S-curve of a new product: "All new products and technologies go through three clear stages of growth . . . It takes the same time for a new technology or product to go from 0 to 10 percent (Innovation phase) of its potential market as it does from 10 to 90 percent (Growth phase) and as it does from 90 to 100 percent (Maturity phase)." The following figure depicts a typical S-curve.

Dent used the development of the automobile to illustrate his point.

When the first automobiles appeared in the late 1890s and early 1900s, no one took them seriously. People laughed at the "horseless carriages" and considered them toys for the rich rather than serious transportation. By 1914, at the end of the innovation phase, only 10 percent of urban families could afford to buy a car.

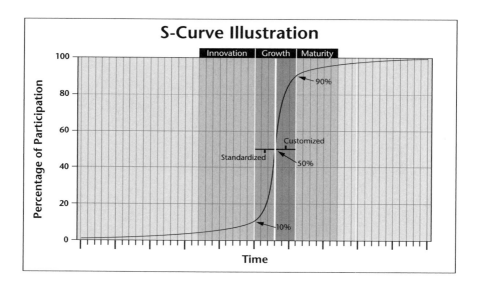

In 1914, Henry Ford developed a standardized design—the Model T—making it easier, more efficient, and less expensive to manufacture his cars. This marked the beginning of the growth phase, which consists of two equal segments: standardization and customization. As Dent explained, it takes as long for a product to go from 10 to 50 percent of the market (standardization) as it does to go from 50 to 90 percent (customization). Ford's moving assembly line refined his process for building high-quality, standardized cars. Seven years later, in 1921, roughly 50 percent of urban families owned their own cars. That's when General Motors began customizing cars by offering different models and colors. Seven years after that, in 1928, the growth phase ended and 90 percent of American families owned automobiles.

After 1928, the automobile industry entered the maturity phase. Cars were totally accepted as part of American society. Installment financing and automobile-related industries swept the country, making this, in Dent's words, "the century of the car."

Although Dent believes it takes the same amount of time to go from one phase to the next, that's not always the case. The following figure shows an S-curve applied to the rock and roll

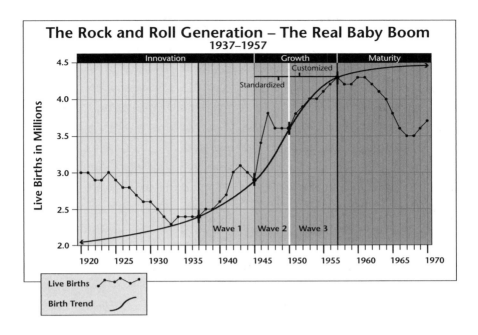

The Rock and Roll Generation – The Real Baby Boom
1937–1957

generation's birth waves. As you can see, the growth phase was shorter than the innovation and maturity phases.

The Rock and Roll Generation Comes of Age

Interestingly, Dent's three phases also apply to the counter-cultural revolution that took place as the rock and roll generation came of age. Let's examine some of the events that occurred and the people who were largely responsible for them.

The Innovation Phase (born prior to 1945)

People born in 1938 and 1939 had a radically different outlook from people born just a few years earlier. The preceding "baby bust" generation, born from 1926 through 1933, was very small. Those kids grew up during the depression and World War II—cataclysmic events that dramatically affected their personalities. In contrast, the earliest rock and rollers grew up in the 1950s, during relatively good economic times. Too young to remember World

War II, they came of age socially in the early 1960s.

Unfortunately, those first rock and rollers had a major identity crisis. As youth, they had no real role models because their upbringing and early life experiences were vastly different from the previous generation's. Like the early automobiles, this group was fragmented, with many ideas about who and what they could be, but no real consensus. However, just as the fragmented start of the automobile led to the transportation revolution, the rock and rollers' search for identity eventually led to the countercultural revolution of the 1960s.

Almost without exception, the leaders of the countercultural revolution were born prior to 1946. These role models included personalities as diverse as Malcolm X, Hugh Hefner, Martin Luther King Jr., Gloria Steinem, and Muhammad Ali. In the popular arts, first-phase innovators included Andy Warhol, Elvis Presley, Buddy Holly, Dennis Hopper, Peter Fonda, Frank Zappa, Bob Dylan, Joan Baez, Twyla Tharp, all four Beatles, Jimi Hendrix, Janis Joplin, Jim Morrison, John Denver, "Mama" Cass Elliott, and Mick Jagger. Though you may disagree with some of their radical ideas, these individuals were agents of change and their contributions immeasurable. They introduced concepts that others adopted.

The Growth Phase (born 1945 to 1957)

This second group endorsed and spread the countercultural revolution started by the innovators. They jumped on the bandwagon (or in their case, the Volkswagen bus) and caused the movement to grow and evolve.

Before we go any further, I want to emphasize that not all members of this second group bought into the new culture. During the first half of the growth phase, when the standardization segment (born between 1945 and 1950) came of age, only about half of them participated in the countercultural revolution, just as only half of all car buyers owned Model Ts during the standardization segment of the automobile's development.

With their long hair, bell-bottom jeans, wide belts, and tie-dyed T-shirts, this standardization group seemed to have come from a single mold. They spoke the same language ("Far out, man") and thought the same thoughts. They were anti-war, anti-establishment, pro-peace, and pro-sex. It didn't matter if they were wealthy or poor, college educated or high school dropouts, their ideology was the same: Peace and love! Sex, drugs, and rock and roll!

Although they weren't the innovators, members of the growth phase had greater impact (and often receive all the credit) because their numbers dwarfed the previous group's. Take Woodstock, for example. Most people consider the 1969 music concert and festival to be the "coming out party" of the baby boom generation. The real leaders, though—almost all the performers appearing on stage—were actually born during the innovation phase.

The second half of the growth phase, the customization segment, took place during the 1970s, as the group born between 1950 and 1957 came of age. Thanks to the pioneering efforts of those who'd gone before them, this group had it relatively easy. When it was time for them to go to school, they went to brand-new facilities that had been built for the previous group. When it was time to buy their first cars, they knew they wanted either a Mustang or a Camaro, because that's what the older kids drove. The customized half of the growth phase knew how to dress and which records to buy—their style was predetermined for them. They simply moderated many ideas from the earlier phases, bringing them into the mainstream. Everything the older kids did was now becoming "the way."

The Maturity Phase (born after 1957)

By the time this last group came of age, the Vietnam War was over and the stock market was rebounding from its 1974 low. This group grew up, went to work, got married, and raised their families in a society that had been radically altered by the countercultural revolution. America had moved from a structured, industrial economy to the new information technology. Parents were raising children differently than they'd been raised themselves. Even the workplace was different. The world had become a kinder, gentler, more integrated and inclusive society. It still wasn't perfect, but it had certainly come a long way since the 1960s.

A Generation of Continual Change

At the beginning of this chapter, I disagreed with those who gloomily predict the fall of our economy. They fail to consider not only the power and determination of the rock and roll generation, but also our sheer size and associated financial impact. *Beyond 50: A Report to the Nation on Consumers in the Marketplace* (AARP, 2004) found that Americans age 45 and older are responsible for more than half of all consumer spending—and our market share is growing as our generation ages.

For almost six decades, we've not only influenced our culture and society, our tastes have also driven the American economy, and it's not very likely that our buying power will have any less influence in the coming years. As we became potential customers, it didn't take manufacturers and advertisers long to realize that the surest pathway to success was by meeting our desires. For example:

- In the late 1940s, the demand for baby foods went through the roof. The late 1940s and 1950s also saw toy manufacturing become a growth industry.

- Acne medicine and car sales boomed in the 1960s and early 1970s.

- We drove growth in housing in the late 1970s and 1980s.

- When we finally began putting money aside for the future in the mid 1980s and 1990s, financial services grew and prospered.

From diapers and baby foods to luxury cars and gourmet dinners, if we liked it or needed it, large numbers of us (or our parents) bought it.

As we grew up, the vast numbers of children in the rock and roll generation also required significant changes in the education system. As we reached school age, we caused revolutions in school construction, teacher training, numbers of high school graduates and college attendees, and even theories of child development.

As our large population bubble worked its way through the economy, we imposed our values and beliefs on the rest of America. Back in the 1960s, the oldest segment of the rock and roll generation created a whole new paradigm, a cultural revolution. They led the civil rights movement, demanded voting reform, and propelled the women's movement. After witnessing Vietnam, they pressured the government to end the peacetime military draft in 1973. Responding to John F. Kennedy's call, they joined the Peace Corps, Vista, and other nonmilitary service organizations and brought a new meaning to the term *national service*. In short, they demanded change and they got it. Their revolutions for tolerance, equality, and fairness determined the standard for today. Now they're about to do it again.

Just as they did in those earlier years, a small percentage of people from the innovation phase are leading the way—and it won't be long before their way becomes the norm. As they navigate their 60s, these innovators have already begun paving the way for the next revolution. They're changing our view about aging, life after 50, and the concept of "older Americans" forever. It's no overstatement to say that the leaders of this generation will reinvent retirement before they're done.

Rethinking Retirement

"We should all retire at the end of each day to rest and begin anew.
We should never retire from life."
—Dr. Craig Overmyer, life vision coach

Like many people in his generation, my dad spent 40 years with the same employer, counting the days until he retired. The big day finally came when he was 62 years old. He started collecting Social Security benefits, his mortgage was paid in full, and he received a nice pension—a profit-sharing plan that he rolled into his IRA. Like many of his cohorts, he found it easy to downsize, and he'll have no problem staying financially independent for the rest of his life.

Our generation faces a different kind of future. Unlike our parents, many of us have changed jobs and careers a number of times over the years. We don't have the same pension and profit-sharing plans they had, and Social Security may not be available. Financially, it might not make sense to pursue traditional retirement.

Besides, we rock and rollers don't think the way our parents did. Thanks to breakthroughs in science, medicine, nutrition, and technology, most of us will enjoy good health and strength for many years to come. At age 50, we look and feel better than our parents did at 30. Heck, I'm physically stronger and I feel better at 50 than I did at 30, and so do many of my friends. We easily identify with baseball legend Satchel Paige, who asked, "How old would you be if you didn't know how old you were?"

Plenty of rock and rollers are living a lifestyle we love, and we don't want it to end. We never want to be "over the hill." We want to believe that if we do things right, we'll keep getting better and living profitably for decades longer than our parents imagined. We aren't willing to postpone enjoyment until we retire. We want to build balance into our lives *now,* enjoy ourselves today, and continue that lifestyle for many years to come. Why should we wait all week to say, "Thank God it's Friday"? We want *every* day to feel as good as the weekend. With our kids grown and our careers at their peak, we're approaching a time in life when we only have to be responsible for ourselves. At this stage of life, our biggest concern can and should be, How will we maintain our quality of life and make it even better?

To get a different result than the older generation got, we'll have to revolutionize the way we address that question. Pat, a good friend and client of mine, did exactly that.

Pat's hobby was flying airplanes, and he just loved to fly. Over the years, after adding a commercial license and an instrument rating, he decided to take his flying to the next level. He got his instructor's license and began teaching a few lessons here and there. A couple of years ago, he came to me and said, "You know, Tom, I think I can supplement my income by teaching flying lessons when I retire. I'd like to build that into my plan."

Pat's plan worked out even better—and sooner—than he expected. Several months ago, he was given an opportunity to take early retirement at age 55. His company, like so many others, was doing a little downsizing. They offered Pat a severance package, if he wanted to use it.

The first thing Pat did was go to the airport and talk to the management about the possibility of teaching. They said, "Pat, we'd love to have you. As a matter of fact, you can do it full time if you'd like and head the flight school. We have an office upstairs and you're welcome to it." Pat then came to me and we reviewed his portfolio. He'd done a good job of saving over the years, and we felt that an early retirement supplemented with instructor's pay made perfectly good sense. So Pat accepted the package and said good-bye to his former career.

The next morning, Pat's was the first car in the parking lot and the last to leave that night, and that's pretty much the way it's been ever since. Pat's living his dreams and loving his life. He's doing exactly what he wanted to do. He's even doing customer contract flying all around the Midwest. As time goes on, he may get burned out teaching as many lessons as he is right now, but it will be easy for him to adapt his schedule, change his hours, and pursue his other interests.

If people like Pat are any indication of things to come, transitions like his will become much more prevalent. It's likely that many of us will *not* leave our jobs, our homes, and our friends to retire to sunny communities and vegetate for two or three decades.

Instead, research indicates that many of us intend to work during our "retirement" years, remaining vibrantly active and financially self-sufficient.

The old way was to go to school, work, retire, and die. I see a future with a more cyclical lifestyle: We'll work at one career for a while, then start new careers (part- or full-time) or maybe our own businesses. I see a future in which we'll run through several cycles: learn, work, adapt, take a break; then go back to school and learn, work, adapt again.

I see a future in which rock and rollers won't retire to a life of boredom and unrewarding activities; we'll simply move forward from our existing positions. For many of us, semiretirement will become a viable option. Instead of the all-or-nothing approach taken by the previous generation, we might cut back our hours and spend more time doing what we love and loving what we do.

I see a future in which we'll use our knowledge, skills, and insights to become productive in exciting new ways—starting second or third careers, pursuing our calling in life, or turning a hobby into a revenue source. Maybe we'll take a sabbatical for a year or two in our 50s or early 60s to rethink our lives and redis-cover our purpose. Maybe we'll go back to school and learn new skills or develop untapped passions.

I see a future in which corporations will change their models to accommodate this aging generation. We have a lot of skills and knowledge to offer and will for years to come. I envision corpo-rations moving away from the traditional 40-hour workweek and letting rock and rollers customize their work schedules to focus on the areas they're most passionate about and in which they think they can add the most value. Companies that fail to adapt will see a brain drain as we leave those firms, begin our own start-up businesses, and create new cutting-edge services and ideas.

Human creativity doesn't have to end at some arbitrary age. If we're savvy, those of us who want to work will be able to choose the type and duration, not by our calendar age, but by our health, physical condition, personal disposition, desire, and a host of more important factors. We'll be able to reshape the work we do into a variety of innovative and attractive forms, including part-time work, job sharing, and new business ventures.

A Call to Action

A potentially exciting future for our generation doesn't automatically mean an exciting future for *everyone*. To take an active part in the excitement by shaping the future means deciding *now* how we're going to do it. And that means setting some goals.

Experience teaches us three things about accomplishing goals:

1. Almost nothing worthwhile happens without planning.
2. Successful planning is often a matter of having an accurate picture of where we want to go, then developing a road map of intermediate, attainable goals to get there.
3. The best outcomes are usually achieved over time rather than overnight.

Knowing this, many of us still put off planning for our later years. Why? Perhaps we've been seduced by our own youthful appearance and health; after all, we spend a lot of money and effort keeping the ravages of aging away from our bodies and brains. Of course, there's nothing wrong with appearing and feeling youthful—unless it keeps us from preparing for the future that will inevitably arrive.

Don't let that happen to you. Don't act your age—*plan* your age! You've heard the old saying: To get the same results as everyone else, do exactly what they did. If you want to age like many people of the older generation did, just follow in their footsteps—retire in your 60s, sit on the couch and watch TV or work the crossword puzzle, go to the same restaurant every week for the early bird special, and take vacations to the same place every year. That may work for them, but if you want a different result, you'll have to do something different. Make a radical change. Join the revolution. Think counterintuitively.

To make life after 50 your best years yet, three things are required: a compelling vision of your future life, the financial freedom to pursue your interests, and a sense of health and vitality. Attaining all three is easy when you follow the seven keys to total wealth and abundance. They're the same keys I practice in personal wealth management. By applying them to your finances and other areas of life, you'll quickly discover how easy it is to maximize your wealth and live an abundant life.

If you're ready to discover the seven keys, you'll find them in chapter 2. But before you go any further, here's your first set of coaching questions to get you thinking about life after 50 and the amazing possibilities it holds for you. You'll find similar questions at the end of each chapter. Don't worry, this isn't some time-consuming homework assignment. You don't even have to write anything down, unless you want to. Just take a minute or two to think about your answers. Let your imagination soar like it did when you were a kid, have fun, and enjoy the process.

◆ ◆ ◆

Coaching Questions

Are You Ready for the Next Revolution?

- For most people, the first 50 years were fairly predictable. You went to school, graduated, started your career, and raised a family.

  What's next? What's waiting on your horizon for life after 50?

- At age 50, you probably look and feel better than your parents did at 30.

  How will you keep it going? What's your plan for staying physically healthy and vital?

- Remember, almost nothing worthwhile happens without careful planning.

  Do you have an accurate picture of where you want to go? Do you have a road map of attainable intermediate goals to get you there?

Chapter 2

SEVEN KEYS TO TOTAL WEALTH AND ABUNDANCE

Twenty years ago, in 1984, a young commercial airline pilot decided he needed a financial plan. With roughly $50,000 in investments, a house, and a small piece of rental property, Fred's net worth was just over $138,000. His wife, a full-time homemaker, was pregnant with their second child. Fred's earnings as a pilot would be their only income.

Today, at age 49, Fred's net worth is $3.6 million and growing. More important, he's living a life he loves. He still works at a career he's always enjoyed; he has time for his hobbies and interests; and he's an integral part of a happy, loving family. The results he achieved may sound spectacular, but Fred simply followed the seven keys to total wealth and abundance you're about to learn in this chapter—seven simple steps that anyone can use.

Fred's Story

Even as a young pilot, Fred wisely understood that, at any point in time, he was only "one medical exam away" from the end of his career. He'd seen other pilots develop illnesses or injuries that grounded them for life, and he wanted to be prepared in case it happened to him. He knew how fickle his industry could be—if business was down, large groups of pilots and flight attendants could be furloughed (temporarily laid off) at a moment's notice.

He also knew that the key to his family's security was money.

Before we go any further, let's tackle this sometimes awkward subject head-on. *Money.* What do you think of when you hear that word? Were you taught, like many people, that money is the root of all evil? Money can't buy happiness? Money talks? Money corrupts? Money doesn't grow on trees? Many people are uncomfortable with the topic. They don't like to think about it, much less talk about it or make it a priority in their lives. As a result, they often procrastinate when it comes to making financial decisions.

As you learned in the last chapter, life after 50 can be your best years yet—*if* you focus on three important areas: a compelling vision for your future, financial freedom, and your health and vitality. In other words, to make life after 50 your best years yet, you're going to have to think about money. It's not the only thing, and it may not be the most important thing, but it ranks right up there in the top three.

As you read this book, you'll be asked to let go of any limiting beliefs you may have about money. What's a limiting belief? It's a thought or idea that holds you back and keeps you from accomplishing your goals and dreams. Such beliefs may be unconscious or subconscious, but they're powerful detractors and they definitely exist. For instance, if you have even a vague, nagging belief that money is negative in any way, you may have found yourself doing subtle things throughout your life that interfered with your saving, investing, or financial success. Before you read any further, please take a moment or two and think about your beliefs about money. What's the first thing that pops into your mind when you think of that word? What were you taught about money as a child?

If you've been highly successful in dealing with money, you may not uncover any negative beliefs. However, if you do find some, it's time to replace them with a different point of view. I suggest you start thinking of money as a tool; nothing more, nothing less. Consider it a means to an end, an exchange mechanism for buying the financial freedom to pursue your purpose and passion in life. Money buys opportunity. What you do with that opportunity is entirely up to you.

Let's get back to Fred, our pilot friend. He knew the importance of using financial security as a tool to ensure his family's future. He'd already developed two good habits: saving a portion of what he earned and following a budget. His next step was to create a financial plan. When his accountant referred him to me, we arranged a meeting to discuss his concerns.

At the time, I was with a major brokerage firm, and we offered what was then considered state-of-the-art financial planning. After I conducted a lengthy interview with Fred and gathered his financial information, my firm produced a detailed report filled with statistics and long-range projections.

Typically, investment management and financial planning are treated as two stand-alone disciplines. As Fred's financial planner, my role was to focus on gathering his data and producing a one-time written plan. As his investment manager, my job was to manage his assets and watch them grow. Because I was in the unique position of handling both responsibilities, and because I practice the seven keys to total wealth and abundance, merely knowing Fred's financial goals wasn't enough. I also wanted to understand his dreams and life goals and what I could do to help them come true.

Key #1: Take Time to Create a Compelling Vision

*"You will make many journeys. Always keep
your destination in mind or you will never get there."*
—Mahatma Gandhi, Indian leader and humanitarian

With a little coaching, Fred decided he wanted the ability to retire at age 50 if he needed or chose to when the time came. "I didn't actually plan on retiring at 50," he recalled. "I enjoy flying. I always figured I'd work until I had to retire, but we picked age 50 because it provided a cushion, a conservative point to shoot for. I wanted the choice to be able to walk away if I wasn't enjoying where I happened to be working, or if I had medical problems. We picked age 50 just to give me choices at that point."

I encouraged Fred to refine his vision by thinking about what retiring at age 50 might include. What kind of lifestyle would his family want? Where would they live? How much would they need in accumulated assets to generate the income their lifestyle would require? After adjusting for 2004 dollars (the year Fred would turn 50) and the consumer price index, we set a target of just under a million dollars.

You already know Fred achieved his goal. However, I failed to mention that he did it nine years early: Fred reached the million-dollar mark at age 41. By utilizing the seven keys to total wealth and abundance, he not only achieved his goal, he exceeded it several times over.

Over the last 20 years, Fred's portfolio went through all types of markets. There were times when it did great and times when it was down. No matter when I talked to Fred, the bullishness or bearishness of the market never made a difference in his demeanor. He never allowed fear, greed, or the day-to-day and month-to-month market fluctuations to interfere with his investment discipline. Regardless of the market's direction, Fred stayed calm and focused—because he had a vision of being financially independent.

Tap into Visioning Power

I'm sure you've heard about the power of a vision. Athletes tap into it all the time. They see themselves making the shot, scoring the goal, shattering the record. For athletes, visioning means rehearsing their future success over and over in their minds, and then going out and doing it for real. But what if they had no goals or dreams? What would be the point of playing the game, staying in shape, or working so hard?

You don't have to be an athlete to use visioning power. Here's a simple example Steve Moeller shares in his seminars. Let's say you decide to go horseback riding one day. Pretend you've never been on a horse before, and you just decide to give it a try. Imagine you're riding along, and all of a sudden you fall off the horse. You might exclaim, "That wasn't fun. Horseback riding means getting hurt. That's it for me. I've had enough."

Now let's roll back the clock and try it again—this time with a vision in mind. Suppose you decide to take up horseback riding because you think you'd like to try championship show jumping. You envision yourself in exciting competitions, taking one hurdle after another on the back of a sleek, powerful horse. Armed with your vision, you step into the training ring on that very first day, ride for a few minutes, and fall off the horse. (You didn't think having a vision would make you an expert on your first try, did you?) Yes, you still fall off. But this time, instead of calling it quits, you say, "I guess I have a lot to learn. I'll get back on and try something different so I can make my dream come true."

A compelling vision can mean the difference between climbing back into the saddle or sitting in a miserable heap on the ground. Without a vision, past experience becomes the default position.

Why Vision?

My grandfather once told me, "Tommy, if I'd known I was going to live this long, I would have taken better care of myself." Like many people of his generation, he had no idea he would get so old and feel so bad. After all, hardly anyone in his parents' and grandparents' generations had lived very long. With the average life expectancy going from 47 to 75 in the last 100 years, old age probably took many people by surprise. Key #1 is about keeping that from happening to you. By creating a compelling vision of your future life, you can take steps now to make that vision possible.

Of course, there are always those who say, "Why should I waste my time thinking about the future? I could get hit by a bus tomorrow." That's true, and I won't deny it. Anything's possible— it's just not very probable. As a technical analyst, I look closely at probabilities. Statistically, it's highly unlikely that many of us will be hit by buses or killed in other calamitous ways. Since it's far more likely that we'll live to be old, the real question isn't whether or not we'll be alive in the future, but how will we feel and what will we do when we get there? I don't know about you, but I don't want to end up like Grandpa Pratt, surprised to be alive and wishing I'd done things differently when I had the chance. I'd rather take time to vision about the future and put the wheels in motion to create some possibilities.

When I talk to people about this concept of visioning, many say, "I can't do it. I don't know how to see pictures in my mind." Whether you realize it or not, everything you've ever accomplished came from a vision. Even something as simple as going to the grocery store begins as an idea you play out in your mind. Before you can do any shopping, you have to think about getting in the car, turning the key, driving to the store, picking up what you need, and going home again. After a few times, it becomes so mechanical that you may not know you're doing it, but you're visioning just the same.

Kids vision all the time. Of course, they don't call it visioning; they call it daydreaming. They're just playing games that require imagination. They play house, school, or my old favorites—army man, karate guy, and Major League baseball star. I remember standing in right field in my Little League uniform and dreaming that I was Mickey Mantle. In reality, I was probably playing right field because I wasn't very good. At that age, balls only get to right field when a left-handed hitter comes to the plate, and that doesn't happen too often. But in my mind, I was out in right field because I was Mickey Mantle, leading the Yankees to victory.

Visioning doesn't stop when you hit adolescence. Teenagers dream about their wedding days, they imagine what it will be like to raise a family. They see themselves having careers, becoming war heroes, or being the first to set foot on Mars. They spend countless hours envisioning the things they'll accomplish in life.

As people get older, it seems like their options become fewer and their visions farther apart. As they get married, enter the job market, and have children of their own, they begin to believe certain things just aren't feasible. They focus on their careers and making more money, believing those things will make them happy. It seems the more they work, the less they dream. And when they do think about the future, some of their visions are more like nightmares.

As I conducted research for this book and interviewed people about living longer, I received some surprisingly negative reactions. Over and over I heard, "I don't want to get older if it means losing my health," and "I wouldn't want to outlive my children." Henry, a 72-year-old retiree, told me, "You're just a second away from a stroke anytime in your life, and that can severely alter all your plans." Henry's a great guy, but responses like his are rooted in fear. They're based on a negative vision of old age. They stem from a paradigm that says aging is bad and growing older means pain. This outdated paradigm says if we live to be old, we'll outlive family and friends, run out of money, lose our freedom, and have to keep working at jobs we don't love.

The only thing worse than having no vision at all is having a negative vision. Breaking free of that negative paradigm requires counterintuitive thinking. It starts by accepting the possibility of a different point of view.

Instead of seeing yourself declining, what if you viewed life after 50 as the best years yet? What might happen if you pictured yourself staying pretty much the way you are now, or getting even better for many years to come? What if you believed you could have more fun, more freedom, and more flexibility than at any other time in your life? What if you realized you won't be the only one getting older—increased longevity will affect everyone, and you won't necessarily lose the ones you love? Those would be pretty powerful visions, wouldn't they? They might even compel you to behave in more positive ways today, creating the possibility to make your dreams come true.

That's what Fred did when he started thinking about being able to retire at age 50. He began with a vision of the life he could have, using the same techniques you'll learn when you get to chapter 3.

Key #2: Connect Your Vision to Your Values, Passion, and Purpose

"When you live your purpose, energy flows."
—Sheva Carr, Executive Director, Sunflower Children's Foundation

Unless Fred's vision was closely aligned with what he valued most in life, sustaining and achieving it would have been difficult to impossible. Fortunately, Fred's values supported his vision, making its achievement seem nearly effortless.

Among his most cherished values, Fred includes security, family, independence, and adventure. Being an airline pilot offered plenty of adventure, but it was a little short on the security side. From the beginning, he knew his career had an expiration date—mandatory retirement at age 60. He also knew that injury or physical problems could ground him at any age.

Rather than give up something he was passionate about, Fred found a way to pursue the adventurous career he loved while creating the security he valued so highly. "Even when I was 20," he said, "I was looking forward, projecting to age 50. I knew I had a limited amount of time, so I just worked backward from there."

Both Fred and his wife were willing to save in the present to make their future secure. In fact, that value was so important to both of them that they'd started saving together even before they were married. "When we were very young," Fred recalled, "my wife and I were both very motivated to save and become independent. When we got married, we had money in the bank and we've always made it a priority to set aside a major chunk of our income to put into investments. We've never taken any money out of the accounts that were earmarked as long-term investment accounts. There was obviously something in our character that motivated us to be independent and secure."

As time went by, the couple continued making decisions based on their values, passion, and purpose in life. "Because we were both family oriented and thinking in terms of providing for the family," Fred remembered, "concerns such as having the right amount of life insurance and setting aside funds to provide for the children all rolled together into common goals for us. By setting the money aside and working to assure that the funds would be available at retirement, we also experienced the benefits of having additional choices and increased independence."

As a pilot, Fred has the option of "bidding" for flights. Since different routes involve higher or lower pay, his choices affect his income. International flying, for example, pays more than domestic but it's harder on the body and requires more time away from home. Once again, Fred relies on his vision and values to help him make those kinds of decisions. "Earlier in my career," he said, "I kept an eye on my income stream. As I got closer to the goals and got more comfortable with the fact that I was achieving them, I started bidding schedules that provided more time at home, even though the consequence was less money generated. Had I not started saving and investing early, I'd be scrambling at this point in my life to try to accumulate extra money to be able to invest. Instead, I have more time off to enjoy my family and life away from work."

Fred's story shows how easy it is to stay focused on your vision when it's aligned with your values, passion, and purpose. George, a 67-year-old anesthesiologist and another of my clients, went through a somewhat lengthier process because his values weren't quite as clear to him.

George had always loved growing orchids. Before retiring completely from his anesthesiology practice, he scaled back to part-time hours and started his own greenhouses. Three years later, he retired completely from his practice and turned his hobby into a full-time business.

"Getting into the commercial side of the orchid business became more of a chore than a pleasure," he recalled. "It lost a lot of the fun that it had when it was a hobby." George described "the hassles of trying to maintain the greenhouses, keep up with the lab work, and get decent help. I enjoyed going to the shows," he said, "but I was out in the greenhouses all day long, and it just got to be a big chore." Before he realized it, George found himself working weekends, traveling to orchid shows, and spending time in the lab hybridizing his own breeds. "It took up so much of my time, I didn't have time to enjoy other things," he said. After ten years in the business, he sold his greenhouses and walked away. "Turning a hobby into a career is not always the best thing to do," he concluded.

George's wife, Pat, had been involved with a hospice organization for many years. In fact, she was one of the founders of the facility in her city. George had always been interested in hospices, but was too busy working to ever get involved. "I decided that I'd just get out of the orchid business, since it wasn't fun anymore, and try my hand at hospice work, which I'd always felt was very worthwhile. It just happened that the opportunity was there at the time. The new medical director was very good and he took me under his wing. It was sort of a niche that I fell into, and it really fit well."

Today, four years later, George spends almost as many hours a week at the hospice as he did in the orchid business. He calls himself "a half-time employee working full-time hours." He took the required courses to become certified in hospice and palliative medicine. He's the medical director of the research and education wing of his local hospice. He serves as associate medical director of his city's general hospice, where he provides patient care. He's the physician for the hospice team that covers surrounding rural counties, and he provides direct patient care at the in-patient unit.

Working in the orchid business, George complained that he didn't have time to do other things. Now he works almost as hard but describes himself as happy, fulfilled, and excited about his work. Interesting, don't you think?

George hadn't considered his values before taking either job. In fact, he'd never thought about his values at all, until I interviewed him for this book. When I asked what he thought his most cherished value might be, it didn't take long for George to reply. "I guess it would be contribution," he said. "To be able to make a contribution; to feel like I'm giving back. When I started getting some of my hybrid plants awarded and people were seeking some of those plants, that made me feel like I was contributing something, but not as much as what I feel now." No wonder George loves what he's doing today. It's aligned with his most cherished value in life.

I appreciate George's willingness to share his story, and I hope his candor helps you see the value of aligning your vision with your values, purpose, and passion in life. Using the trial-and-error method, George eventually stumbled across something he loved. There probably aren't any statistics on this, but I'd be willing to bet that the majority of people who try this approach aren't quite as lucky as George finally was. They may spend several years—and vast amounts of money—exploring one idea after another without ever discovering their life's passion. In the next chapter, we'll go through some fun and easy exercises to help you avoid that lengthy process and discover your values, passion, and purpose much more quickly and easily.

Key #3: Educate Yourself and Find a Great Coach

There's an old saying: You can learn from your own experience or benefit from someone else's. As you've probably guessed by now, I recommend the latter. If you want to learn something new or improve your existing skills, there's just no substitute for a good coach.

Please notice that I used the term *coach,* not *teacher, trainer,* or other similar word. That choice was no accident, and I didn't use it just because it's the buzzword of the month. I chose it because I believe life is like a marathon, with healthy longevity as the goal.

Going the distance requires good training, and part of that training is getting good coaching.

Top professionals in all areas of life attribute their success to working with a coach. They know a good coach can help them get results, provide information and knowledge, and bring out the best in them. Coaching shortens the time required, reduces mistakes, and gives them a higher probability of getting what they want.

Fred, our pilot friend, recognized the value of good financial coaching early in his career. "I asked my accountant about financial planning," he said, "because I wanted a professional to help guide us. I believe in seeking guidance and help. I wanted to make sure we weren't making mistakes, that all the areas were covered, and to help make those projections. I probably would have been too aggressive and made bad choices regarding investing."

In the chapters that follow, we'll talk about the value a coach can offer and the qualities to look for in a great coach. We'll explore specific ways a coach can help in crucial areas of life— including exercise, nutrition, finances, and health care.

A coach can help you learn a lot, but before you can choose one, you need a basic understanding of the area in which you want to be coached. Suppose you decided to focus on your physical fitness. Unless you knew a little bit about the different types of exercise, their effects on the body, your own visions and values, and different coaching backgrounds, how would you know who's right for you?

If you wanted to lose weight or develop nutritious habits for life, you'd first need to understand basic nutrition, the benefits and risks of various eating plans, and the types of professionals qualified to help you in this area.

When it comes to your finances and attaining financial freedom, you'd want to understand the fundamentals of investing, how to build net worth, how money actually works, and how it can work for you. Then you'd be ready to identify the person best qualified to help you manage your wealth.

Because each area of life calls for coaches with specific, unique skills, we'll explore those requirements more thoroughly as we discuss each specific area.

Key #4: Formulate and Implement a Measurable Plan

In his book, *Built to Last* (HarperBusiness, 2002), Jim Collins introduced a concept I just love. He called it a BHAG—a big, hairy, audacious goal. BHAGs are like visions, the subject of key #1. They're the wild, crazy dreams that capture your imagination and grab you in the gut. But they shouldn't be confused with key #4: a specific, attainable, measurable plan.

If a vision is the *what,* a plan represents the *how.* Our pilot friend, Fred, had a clear and compelling vision: to be financially independent by age 50. Yet his vision alone wasn't enough. Fred needed a specific plan, consisting of attainable intermediate goals to be reached along the way.

I'm not talking about a typical financial plan, based on numbers and projections that will probably never happen. I'm talking about a plan for amassing the finances to help him attain his *life* vision. Fred's plan listed certain very specific items, like bidding for flights to earn the income he desired, saving a certain amount of money each month, investing it according to a well-thought-out strategy, compiling net worth and cash flow statements to monitor his progress, and always staying focused on his ultimate vision.

Even more important than formulating a plan, Fred actually implemented and followed through on it. This second part of key #4 may seem ridiculously simple, but plenty of people develop plans they never bother to implement. It's a common occurrence in the financial planning arena. I've heard stories from countless individuals who went through the arduous process of gathering their financial documents into a big pile on the kitchen table, hauling them to their advisor's office, then spending several grueling hours filling out extensive and exhausting questionnaires. Eventually, they received a neatly bound booklet with their name on the front and a couple hundred pages of financial reports, depending on their net worth and how large a fee they were willing to pay. The booklet included a cash flow analysis, tax projections, net worth statements, estate plans, and a host of computer-generated projections. After two or three meetings with the advisor, they put the book away on a shelf somewhere and took it down a few years later, only to learn that little, if any, of the information was still relevant.

Don't let this happen to you. Formulating and implementing a plan is the only sure way to achieve your vision for any area of life. As we explore specific life issues in the following chapters, we'll talk about the key components to consider in formulating a plan, as well as some great ideas for following through on the implementation side.

Key #5: Monitor Your Progress and Update the Plan as Needed

There's a common expression in the business world: You can't manage what you don't measure. The saying applies to life as well, and the best coaches tap into its wisdom. When you visit your doctor, she checks your blood pressure, pulse, and respiration rate. When you work with a physical trainer, he measures your muscle mass, body fat, and weight. A nutritionist helps you keep track of the vitamins, minerals, and calories you consume. A personal wealth manager tracks your investments. If they didn't measure your progress, how would you know where you stand?

When it comes to making a plan for any area of life, remember: You can't manage what you don't measure. Keep this in mind from the very beginning, and start by setting measurable goals. If you make the mistake of using general statements like, "I'm going to lose some weight," or "I'm going to get in shape," how will you know whether you're making progress or not? More important, how will you know when you've reached your goal?

Monitoring your progress offers more than just feedback about your results. It lets you know when it's time to update your plan. When a plan isn't working, a slight change here or there can make all the difference in the world. Even better, if your plan's working so well that you're ahead of schedule, as Fred was, measuring it makes you aware of your progress and lets you take advantage of other available options.

"As we saw that we were reaching our goals earlier, we reset the goals," Fred said. "Periodically, I'd set my sights higher, adjusting the dollar amounts I wanted to see at a certain point. When I saw that I was going to reach the goal I had set for age 50 at around age 40, I set new goals. Now I'm approaching age 50 and I still enjoy my job. I have one of the best careers in the industry, so my intention is to continue working and, as long as I stay healthy, work until age 60."

Key #5, monitoring your progress and updating your plan, is one of the most important keys for making life after 50 your best years yet.

Key #6: Enjoy Your Abundance

When I turned 40, and again at 50, I was amazed at the gloomy, depressing messages my birthday cards contained. They said I was "over the hill," and "the worst is yet to come." The message was obvious: Whoever wrote those cards believed that when you reach one of those landmark years, life starts passing you by. That there's a scarcity of time from that point on, and getting older means getting worse.

It's simply not true.

Instead of the win-lose, scarcity thinking that breeds such negativity, I believe in a win-win, prosperity thinking that promises an abundance of time, energy, and vital resources for making life after 50 the best years yet. Thanks to advances in health care, nutrition, medicine, and technology, we have every reason to expect to live and thrive into our 80s, 90s, and beyond. Rather than believing it's all downhill from here, I think the rock and roll generation is about to embrace a whole new paradigm: The best is yet to come, and life after 50 can be more fun than ever.

The internationally renowned author and speaker, Dr. Wayne Dyer, offers another good reason to focus on abundance. In his book *The Power of Intention* (Hay House, 2004), Dyer describes the self-defeating impact of scarcity thinking:

> The way you look at life is essentially a barometer of your expectations, based on what you've been taught you're worthy of and capable of achieving. These expectations are largely imposed by external influences such as family, community, and institutions, but they're also influenced by that ever-present inner companion: your ego. These sources of your expectations are largely based on the beliefs of limitation, scarcity, and pessimism about what's possible for you. If these beliefs are the basis for how you look at life, then this perception of the world is what you expect for yourself. Attracting abundance, prosperity, and success from these limiting viewpoints is an impossibility.

Tapping into your abundance means putting it to good use. When it comes to the concept of wealth, many people are wrapped up in the idea that they need to save, invest, and build their money, while forgetting its real purpose. Money was never intended to be hoarded; it's meant to be used and enjoyed.

In his book, *Good to Great* (HarperCollins, 2001), author Jim Collins introduced a concept he calls "the genius of AND." Collins, a student of enduring great companies, suggests that we "embrace both extremes on a number of dimensions at the same time. Instead of choosing A *OR* B, figure out how to have A *AND* B—purpose *AND* profit, continuity *AND* change, freedom *AND* responsibility." Abundance today and tomorrow.

Not long ago, I met Baseball Hall of Famer Reggie Jackson. He and several of his friends were thinking about buying a corporate jet to use, lease, and make available to others. They figured it would be a pretty good investment. Maybe not in terms of being able to sell for a profit sometime in the future, but because it would add abundance to their lives in the present. Reggie said the jet would save him about a thousand hours per year. Instead of wasting all the time it takes to fly these days, he'd reclaim that time and improve his quality of life.

As you start thinking about how to enjoy your abundance, what could you "invest" in that would add to your life? A digital photography class? Computer training? Golf lessons? A special vacation with your entire family? Yes, there's an expense associated with each of these things, but if you miss out on them, you run into opportunity risk, which financial professionals describe as the risk that a better opportunity may present itself after an irreversible decision has been made.

At the end of the year, your net worth is whatever it is. Opportunity risk refers to the idea that it could have been more if you'd made different decisions. For instance, if you buried your money in the backyard, you missed the opportunity to have it work for you and increase its value.

There's another type of opportunity risk that's usually overlooked: the cost of failing to use your money in ways that enrich the quality of your life. Yes, you need to save and invest for the years ahead, but investing money in yourself can pay big dividends now *and* in the future. What will it cost you in the long run to *not* invest money on these aspects of life? For me, spending quality time with my family and friends, visiting new places, and learning new skills offer far more value to my life than hoarding and saving could ever bring.

Many members of the rock and roll generation are reluctant to invest in themselves this way. They learned from their depression-era parents that something could happen to take away everything they've worked so hard to gain. Fear of the future leads to hoarding, not to rational saving. It causes win-lose thinking as opposed to win-win thinking, scarcity thinking as opposed to abundance thinking.

Fred, the airline pilot we've been following, practiced win-win thinking by working hard, saving money, *and* enjoying the abundance he produced. Even when he was young and saving in a disciplined way, he always had hobbies and enjoyed a good balance in his life. "With ten years still on the horizon to retirement, we're buying more toys and more things for today, because we've done the hard work. We're rewarding ourselves more in this phase of our lives. For many years now, I've had time to take college courses, work in theater and music, and enjoy some great activities with the kids. I built a computer that does digital editing so I can convert videotapes to DVDs and archive all those memories we've created. We're more likely to purchase items we want and to splurge on events our family will enjoy."

Key #6 reminds you to enjoy your abundance by appreciating what you have right now. Most people tend to think about what they don't have, staying focused on their future goals and ignoring the glorious present. Future goals are important, but it's equally imperative to appreciate the abundance you have today. Start by taking stock of what you've accumulated and accomplished in every area of life. Don't take your abundance for granted; enjoy and appreciate it every day.

Key #7: Leave a Lasting Legacy

What do you think of when you hear the word *legacy?* Webster's dictionary defines it as "a gift by will, especially of money or personal property." This definition has been known to send chills down the spines of many otherwise organized individuals. They associate the term with death and dying, and they'd just as soon avoid those topics as long as they possibly can. A client once joked, "My estate plan is to live forever, and so far it's working."

Because of their reluctance to face this uncomfortable subject, many people avoid having their wills drawn up, overlook their insurance needs, and ignore estate planning altogether. They push those items to the back of their minds, where they linger as a nagging reminder of important business they've yet to complete. Some people manage to put these details off for their entire lives, leaving their family and loved ones a legacy of chaos and confusion. Grieving family members end up with hurt feelings, forced to make difficult decisions at an emotional time.

The probabilities are very high that you'll have money and financial assets left over when you reach the end of the proverbial road. What will happen to all those assets you've accumulated during your lifetime? More important, what do you *want* to have happen? Do you really want your 25-year-old children to inherit $3 million? Would they be prepared to handle it, or would the money be better off in some kind of trust, available when they're a little more mature? Do you want to include your alma mater, religious congregation, or some other organization in your estate plan? Would you like to honor someone by making a contribution in his or her honor? These are questions only you can answer, by taking time to consider your present situation and the legacy you want to leave.

Yes, it's difficult to face your own mortality, but these are decisions you really should consider if you want life after 50 to be your best years yet. Your short-term discomfort will quickly be replaced by the peace of mind that comes from knowing you've done all you can to leave a lasting legacy.

Financial bequests aren't the only way to leave your mark upon the world. Who you are and what you do makes an equally powerful impact. Do you remember the classic movie, *It's a Wonderful Life,* starring Jimmy Stewart? He played George Bailey, the savings-and-loan manager who was given a unique opportunity. George got to see what life would have been like if he'd never been born. Like many of us, he'd never stopped to realize that the simple things he did every day affected so many others. Unlike George Bailey, you may never know exactly whom you affect, but you can be sure that you're putting the wheels in motion when you incorporate key #7 into your plan for healthy longevity. In the chapters that follow, we'll look at a number of ways you can apply this key to various areas of life and leave a lasting legacy.

Putting It All Together

Now that you've been introduced to each of the seven keys, it's time to get specific and learn exactly how to apply them. First, let's put them all together for a quick review.

The Seven Keys

1. Take time to create a compelling vision.

2. Connect your vision to your values, passion, and purpose.

3. Educate yourself and find a great coach.

4. Formulate and implement a measurable plan.

5. Monitor your progress and update the plan as needed.

6. Enjoy your abundance.

7. Leave a lasting legacy.

In the next chapter, we'll take a closer look at key #1. Whether you see yourself as an experienced visionary or someone trying it for the very first time, you'll discover a few new tools to try and an assortment of ways to apply them.

❖ ❖ ❖

Coaching Questions

Are You Ready for Total Wealth and Abundance?

- Limiting beliefs are the thoughts and ideas that keep you from accomplishing your goals and dreams.

  What were you taught about money as a child? Do you have any limiting beliefs about money that you need to release?

- By creating a compelling vision of your future life, you can take steps now to make it come true.

  What might happen if you viewed life after 50 as the best years yet? What if you believed you could have more fun, freedom, and flexibility than at any other time in your life?

- Appreciating your abundance means enjoying what you have and putting it to good use.

  What could you "invest" in that would add to your life? What will it eventually cost you not to spend money on those aspects of life?

Chapter 3

VISION, VALUES, PASSION, AND PURPOSE

If you're a fan of western movies, you might remember this scene. A crusty old codger approaches the foreman at the start of a cattle drive. When the codger asks for a job, the foreman just laughs and turns him down flat. He's sure the oldster can't possibly have the stamina or energy to endure the drive.

A few days later, they meet again at the edge of a swollen river. The old man watches the foreman and his men as they futilely attempt to get the cattle across. Finally, the codger approaches the foreman and offers the following proposal: "If I can get the cattle across the river in four hours, will you hire me on for the rest of the drive?" Again, the foreman laughs but promises the old man that the job will be his if he accomplishes the feat by himself.

For the first three hours, the codger does nothing. Then suddenly, he approaches the dominant steer and leads it into the river. Much to the foreman's surprise, the steer begins to swim across. Soon after, all the other cattle follow his lead, and within a few minutes, arrive safely on the opposite shore.

The foreman honors the agreement he made, but just has to know how the old-timer did it. "How did you accomplish single-handedly what all my men could not?" he asks. The old-timer replies, "It was easy. My long experience taught me that no steer will ever swim toward a bank it cannot see. Earlier in the day, the sun shone directly in the cattle's eyes, blinding them and keeping them from seeing the opposite shore. When the sun went down, the cattle could see the other bank and they readily swam toward it."

I hope you'll forgive the comparison, but we humans are a lot like the cattle in this story. Until we can see where we're going, we're reluctant to even start moving.

Dream It, Do It

"You've got to be very careful if you don't know where you're going, 'cause you might not get there."
—Yogi Berra, Baseball Hall of Famer

During your first 50 years, taking time to envision the future might not seem like a worthwhile pursuit. It's much easier to go through life on autopilot, earning money, advancing your career, putting food on the table, and reacting to challenges as they arise.

Ron, a 61-year-old business owner, offered a great description of life before 50. "My goal was always to try to succeed in business," he said, "but when you get there, what do you do next? Where do you go? I don't think I've thought beyond the goal. If you ask a kid, 'What are you striving for?' he says, 'Well, I want to get out of college and I want to get a real good job.' Okay, then what? People don't always think beyond, until they're faced with it."

By the time you reach the half-century mark, you're probably well established in your career and community, your kids are grown or nearly so, and you finally have time to focus on yourself. For some people, the question, Then what? brings on a full-blown crisis. They start thinking life is almost over, and they get depressed because they haven't accomplished what they set out to do. Or worse, they buy into the negative stereotypes about aging and tell themselves, "It's all downhill from here," "The best part of life is behind me," and "It's too late to start anything new."

In his book *Scripts People Live* (Grove/Atlantic, 1990), clinical psychologist Claude Steiner, PhD, explained that people develop early patterns of belief based on the negative or positive influences

of those around them. As a child, you decide, however uncon-
sciously, whether you'll be happy or depressed, a winner or a failure, strong or dependent. Having decided, you spend the rest of
your life making the decision come true. For those who choose a
negative script, the consequences can be disastrous, because negative thoughts do nothing but de-energize and disempower. More
important, they pave the way to a self-fulfilling prophecy. After all,
if you believe it's too late, you won't even try. And if you don't try,
you certainly can't succeed.

If you're living from beliefs that say growing older means deteri-
oration and limitations of your health and wealth, only a conscious
decision to change those beliefs will bring about positive results. In
other words, old, ineffective beliefs invite a future left to chance, but
a compelling vision is like a signpost to a wonderful life.

A Fork in the Road

Try this little exercise and you'll quickly see what I mean. Imagine
you've come to a fork in the road. The signpost on the right reads,
NEW CHOICES. The one on the left says, OLD CHOICES.

Consider the left fork first. Honestly examine any old patterns, tendencies, and beliefs you have about the concept of
aging. Imagine you believed that aging results in less energy
and more limitations. See yourself 5, 10, or 20 years from now,
living from those beliefs. What do you think your life would
be like? Are you afraid you might not have enough financial
resources to sustain you? Would your harmful habits leave you
de-energized and unhealthy? What a frightening picture!

Now, envision the right-hand path. Suppose you made a new
choice to believe that people improve with age. Imagine how
your life would be if, starting today, you did everything in your
power to create a reality of increasing energy and possibilities. See
yourself 5, 10, or 20 years from now, living from your new
beliefs. What would your life be like? What would you be doing
to produce a high quality and length of life, with all the resources

necessary to sustain that vision?

This exercise is about choosing the new, empowering path. By taking a few minutes to go a step further and write down your answers to the preceding questions, you'll begin to experience the power of your choices to envision renewed energy, vitality, and vigor. But that's just the beginning.

- *A compelling vision can dramatically increase your sense of excitement, passion, and enthusiasm for life.* You'll realize you're in charge of your choices and never have to be victimized by life circumstances.

- *A compelling vision creates joy each day as you connect with life's exciting possibilities.* Without a compelling vision, people often project any limiting beliefs and negative experiences from their past into the future, and they fear the unknown. Visioning utilizes your knowledge and wisdom to help you make appropriate decisions about the actions you can take today to create your best possible future.

- *Once you have a compelling vision, decision making is easy.* When your values and vision are clear, you have a criteria for making decisions: *Will taking this action move me toward my vision?* If the answer is no, you'll be less likely to take the action.

- *With a compelling vision, you'll take actions today to create possibilities for your future.* If you envision yourself running a marathon someday, you're not likely to take up smoking today. If you want to retire in the next few years, you probably won't spend every last nickel you have today. However, if you had no idea you wanted to achieve those goals in the future, you might take those actions or even worse ones today.

Turning 50 is a major fork in the road. Without a compelling vision, the path you choose may not seem to make much difference.

With a compelling vision, you'll be pulled down the road toward your future, feeling excited, enthusiastic, and eager to pursue the life you were destined to choose—one with a grand purpose and meaning.

How Visioning Works

People often tell me they don't know how to vision, but visioning is easier than you may think. If I asked you to close your eyes right now and tell me what color shirt you were wearing, could you do it? If so, you can vision. Most people "see" a picture of the shirt in their mind's eye. Others don't, but if they know what color the shirt is, they simply visioned in a nonvisual way. Some people call it remembering. You might call it sensing or feeling. I just happen to use the word *visioning*.

You might be wondering whether this is just the latest self-help mumbo jumbo. Rest assured, visioning is based on real science, and it works because of the way your brain was designed.

First, visioning creates a mental phenomenon called *cognitive dissonance*. Psychologists describe it as the discomfort you feel when you experience an inconsistency between your beliefs and your actions. Smoking is a great example. If you believed that smoking was bad for you, but you smoked anyway, you'd experience cognitive dissonance. The level of discomfort you'd feel would depend on the issue's importance to you and the degree of inconsistency you experienced.

When cognitive dissonance becomes unpleasant enough, it induces a *drive state*—you feel driven to reduce the dissonance by changing either your beliefs or your behaviors. Let's go back to our smoking example. If you smoked, and the dissonance became unpleasant enough, you'd ultimately have to do something about it. You'd either quit smoking or change your beliefs: "Oh, I won't get lung cancer. That only happens to other people."

You may have read stories about wealthy people who've lost all their money, then quickly found ways to become wealthy again.

Conversely, you've probably seen articles about lottery winners who spent or lost their winnings and went back to their previous financial level. They all experienced cognitive dissonance and changed their behaviors to match their beliefs.

Second, the human brain contains a cluster of cells known as the *reticular activating system,* or RAS. This system acts as a filter, sorting out information and sending it to either your conscious or unconscious mind. Can you imagine what life would be like without such a system? Your conscious mind would be bombarded by every stimulus in your environment. You'd hear a sound and not know where to look first—at the chirping bird in a nearby tree, at the children playing in your neighbor's yard, or at the speeding car hurtling toward you.

Fortunately, the RAS filters out the unimportant, or at least puts it in the background. How does your RAS know the difference? It uses your beliefs and values as guidelines. When you decide something's important, your RAS brings it to your attention. For example, if you decided to buy a certain kind of car, you'd suddenly start noticing that model on the road. Or if your first-born daughter just announced that she was pregnant, you'd start seeing pregnant women everywhere you went. When you take time to envision a compelling future, your reticular activating system automatically focuses your attention on the information, opportunities, and resources to help bring that vision to life.

I can't say enough about the powerful impact of using these elements to your advantage. When you formulate a compelling vision, cognitive dissonance recognizes the gap between where you are and where you want to be. The resulting discomfort drives you to take action and bring your reality into alignment with your beliefs. Then your RAS enters the picture, drawing your attention to the people, places, and things that will help you attain your vision in easy, effortless ways. Interestingly, that's exactly what happened to me last year.

Last winter, I slipped on a piece of ice and slightly injured my back. I went to a nurse massage therapist, and while I waited in the reception area, I noticed two books featuring Dr. Craig Overmyer: *Dynamic Health* and *Success Is a Decision of the Mind.* Thumbing through them, I learned that Craig is a Heal*thy* Living Coach who inspires and motivates people to transform their futures by creating a vision of their next level of best. For more than 15 years, Craig counseled clients at St. Vincent's Hospital Stress Center in Indianapolis, Indiana, where he specialized in the power of the belief system to influence health and longevity.

I asked the nurse, "Do you know this guy? I'd like to talk to him," and left her my card. A few days later, Craig called. I nearly dropped the phone when he said, "I worked with a financial planner on a great idea—to integrate life vision coaching with personal finance. I invested a lot of work and am ready to put it into practice." I could hardly believe my ears. Craig described exactly what I wanted to do! Many of my clients are interested in more than just left-brained financial statistics and advice. They want a new kind of conversation with their advisors about using money and tangible items to create choices and enhance the quality of their lives. For quite some time, I'd been envisioning a way to serve that need, and the solution appeared in Craig.

Today, Craig is a valued member of my personal wealth management firm, where he offers life vision coaching to all of our clients. He also contributed much of the material you'll learn in this chapter. None of that would have happened without a compelling vision. Craig had a vision of working with a financial advisor to help people integrate their lives and finances. I had a vision of working with a coach who could guide my clients as they focus on their lives and goals. Although we came from two different disciplines, we instantly saw a connection between them. We had a clear idea of where we were headed and what we wanted to do. Without a vision, I probably wouldn't have given Craig's books a second glance that day.

A Note Before You Start Visioning

Scientists know that the brain is divided into two hemispheres. The analytical left brain deals with numbers, logic, and finite concepts. The creative right brain deals with abstract ideas, fantasy, and imagination; this side knows no limits. Business coach Steve Moeller describes the right brain as the accelerator and the left brain as the brake.

When you vision, be right-brained. See pictures, feel emotions, and think about the possibilities for your life. That might not be easy at first, because people typically use their left brains when reading, but here's a quick tip that really works:

Don't try to speed-read this chapter.

If you see something that interests you, don't feel like you have to plow ahead. Take time to lay the book in your lap, close your eyes, and think about how the information relates to you and your situation. This simple action will move you from left-brain thinking to right-brain visioning. You may want to keep a journal nearby to capture and record some of your thoughts.

Once you create your vision, then you can use your left brain to analyze its possibilities, set goals, and choose appropriate actions. Your left brain will answer the question, What steps should I take to create the possibility for my vision to happen?

Here's another interesting reason to tap into your right brain: It can't tell fact from fiction. Why do you jump out of your seat when you watch a horror movie? Because your right brain doesn't know that the creatures on the screen aren't real. You jump when they lunge toward you, until your left brain reminds you, "It's only a movie." Use this to your advantage and deliberately create some cognitive dissonance. Remember, when you clearly and vividly envision your future, your brain will start taking steps to close the gap between where you are and where you could be.

In the next few pages, you'll learn seven dimensions of the visioning process Craig developed before we met. Amazingly, these dimensions have a lot in common with my seven keys. Ideally, these exercises are best done with a coach—someone who can guide you and help you explore the possibilities within yourself. If you don't have someone like that available, invite a trusted friend or family member to be your partner and do the exercises together. Some of the exercises are also available at www.nevertooold.com.

Whichever method you choose, have fun, dream with an open mind, and connect with visions that will inspire and empower you to make life after 50 your best years yet.

The Greatest Treasure Hunt of Your Life

"But that is not treasure for us which another man has lost;
rather it is for us to seek what no other man
has found or can find."
—Henry David Thoreau, American author and philosopher

Expanding yourself to create a vision of possibilities is like embarking on a treasure hunt. Imagine yourself on a majestic ship, in search of buried treasure. What's the first thing you'll need? A map, of course. A compelling vision is the map to your life's destination. Once you know where you want to go, you can plot your course and prepare for dangers that might arise. With the wind in your sails and a sturdy main mast (your most cherished values), you'll be able to set short-term goals, develop timelines, and enjoy the journey. Upon arriving, you'll celebrate your good fortune and share it with others.

The following questions will guide you on your treasure hunt. Remember, be right-brained and don't be distracted by the whys and hows. Your left brain will get its turn later. Are you ready to start? Then let the voyage begin!

1. What Are the Possibilities for Your Life?

If you're going on a treasure hunt, you need a map and you need to decide where you're going. The map can't choose for you;

it just shows you the possibilities. In the same way, your inner treasure hunt begins by considering the wholeness of life—looking at all the possibilities from the biggest perspective.

Sometimes your perspective can become very small. Consider this: If our galaxy, the Milky Way, was put onto a huge map the size of the state of Rhode Island, our whole solar system, with the sun and all the planets, would be just a pinpoint on that map. That's the kind of perspective you get when you think about the grandeur of life and how precious it is to be alive. In a similar way, this first guideline is about stretching your awareness of all the possibilities available to you. Don't be a scarcity thinker and limit yourself to just one or two choices in life; be an abundance thinker, look at the bigger picture, and you'll discover innumerable options.

First, take stock of all your assets, all the tangibles and intangibles that comprise your real wealth. Appreciate everything you already have—everything that's *good* in your life. Consider your total wealth; not just your finances, but all areas of life. Look at your health, your physical fitness, your relationships, your career, your hobbies, and everything that matters to you. Don't forget to include the good or knowledge you've gained from events you once viewed as negative. You'll quickly discover that you're surrounded by an abundance of treasures.

Next, examine any areas where your life feels out of balance. Maybe you've built a great career but now want to head in a different direction. Perhaps you had some values in the past that are now obsolete. Are there things in your life that you wish you could change?

At age 50, Wes was the president and chief operating officer of an auto body paint distributing company. He'd been brought in to turn the business around, and after doing so, started feeling a little bored. He examined the possibilities for his future life and made a radical decision. "The company's doing well, and we report record earnings," he said, "but this isn't what I want to do. It's not going to change unless I take the initiative."

Wes and his wife had talked for some time about spending more time in Arizona, where their son lived. Doing some right-brain visioning, Wes realized that if he could reduce his work hours by a third, they'd be able to bring their vision to life. He let his left brain kick in and came up with a plan: "Because I'm still working for the company, doing things that need to happen every week, I can't work two months and take a month off. So what I've figured out is, I take off every Friday, every other Thursday, and one more day a month. I love that."

Now it's your turn. What's your vision for your future life? What are all the possibilities you could explore? Let your right brain run totally wild and answer the following questions:

- How would you define a wealthy life?
- If you didn't have to work for a living, what would you do?
- What are you passionate about or highly interested in?
- If money were no object, what kind of lifestyle would you live?
- What would you do to be your best for the world?

2. What's Your Purpose?

The first guideline was about exploring the map and considering all the possibilities available to you. This second guideline is about deciding which destinations you'll visit on your treasure hunt. It's about having clear intentions of the life you want to have and create. Even if you don't get what you want, be open to the possibility of getting what you need and expecting support.

Thomas Parker Emery is a renowned sculptor and painter. He's sculpted U.S. presidents, university officials, and countless other dignitaries. At age 81, he still arrives at his studio first thing every morning and spends a few hours sketching. He teaches a handful of private students and continues to work professionally. Emery doesn't have a job or a career; he has a calling that reflects his purpose in life.

As a Boy Scout, young Tom needed to earn merit badges and thought art might be fun. "I don't know why. I just wanted an art merit badge," he recalled. "I didn't know I could draw or anything." He couldn't earn the badge at school—his school didn't even offer art—so he went to his scoutmaster for advice. "Tom," the scoutmaster suggested, "why don't you take something practical, some merit badge you can use?" Emery was undeterred, so the scoutmaster referred him to the local art merit badge counselor, a Mr. Silvermail, who lived on a farm some distance away. It took Tom all day to find the place. When he finally pedaled his bike to the top of the hill where the Silvermails lived, his arrival was greeted with some surprise. "For heaven's sakes!" Mr. Silvermail exclaimed, "I've been an art merit badge counselor for 25 years and you're the first one who ever came here."

As their relationship progressed and Emery's talent became apparent, Mr. Silvermail sponsored his attendance at a school where he'd have a chance for a scholarship. Emery earned the scholarship and went on to become the respected sculptor he is today. And all because a persistent young boy felt compelled to pursue something new.

As you consider your purpose in life, keep in mind the distinction between a job, a career, and a calling. A *job* is the penalty you pay to get the money to have the life you want. No one likes a job. A *career* is fun, it's part of your identity, but it can also burn you out. At some point, you master your career; the journey's not over but it becomes a bit routine. A *calling* is your heart's desire, your life's purpose, something you're passionate about. Have you ever noticed that people with a calling rarely think about retiring? People like Thomas Emery, Mother Teresa, and Dr. Jonas Salk pursued their heart's desire and seemed to enjoy the journey every step of the way.

Like them, each of us was created with a grand design for a purposeful existence. Those who know their purpose and have a plan to actively pursue it experience true fulfillment. However, many people have a tough time putting their purpose into a few words, or haven't taken time to figure it out. Here are some questions to help you discover your purpose and passions in life:

- What do you do best (your innate talents and gifts)?
- If you could be best in the world at something, what would it be?
- What drives you most strongly (what are your convictions)?
- If you could accomplish anything you wanted and knew you could not fail, how would you spend your time?
- Ask the people who know you well, "What do you think are my strongest attributes? What do you like most about me?"

3. What Old, Ineffective Patterns Could Sabotage Your Treasure Hunt?

Dr. David Oeschger, a clinical psychologist, identifies two different kinds of people: fear-based and opportunity-based. The fear-based individual expects disaster around every corner. The opportunity-based person sees every problem as an opportunity.

One of Dr. Oeschger's clients was a fear-based fellow who really hated his job. Every Sunday night, the poor guy's stomach would tie up in knots, anticipating Monday morning. This man was a highly trained, highly skilled individual who'd worked at his company for quite some time. Quitting to take another job would mean a severe pay cut, so our unfortunate friend felt trapped. Then his company started laying people off, and the man became more fearful than before.

Oeschger told him, "If the worst thing happens and you get laid off, you'll be forced to do the thing you won't do now, which is get another job. You're afraid to take that step because it would reduce your salary. Have you considered the fact that you might be a lot happier? Isn't your personal happiness more important than a certain level of income?" Ultimately, the man was laid off. As

Oeschger predicted, he coped with it, got another job, and wound up happier than before.

As this example illustrates, old, ineffective patterns of thought and action can sabotage your wealth and health. Henry Ford once said, "Whether you think you can or you think you can't, you're right." When your beliefs change, your behaviors change.

If you're on a ship making a journey, you need to look for the danger zones—the patterns and beliefs that can wreck your ship. Beware of the three treacherous pirates who want to steal your map: doubt, disappointment, and rejection.

Who among us hasn't been forced to deal with one or more of these de-energizers at some point in life? Discovering your purpose becomes more difficult when you let yourself be trapped by these three. Surrender ineffective worrying, fretting, and regret. Let go of old patterns of thought, speech, and action that are no longer effective. A firm commitment to your vision will give you the courage to relentlessly align yourself with your highest purpose and the grand design for your life.

- What could cause your ship to wreck as you seek your treasure?

- What habitual experiences from your past are limiting your success and happiness?

- What old, ineffective patterns or beliefs could rob you of a wealthy life?

- What patterns or beliefs are blocking your experience of dynamic health and energy?

- What new and empowering beliefs could you adopt instead of the old, ineffective ones?

4. Which of Your Most Cherished Values Will Sustain You on Your Treasure Hunt?

As you embark on your voyage, you'll need a strong mast for

your ship. When building a main mast, shipbuilders choose the tallest, strongest tree they can find. Then they cut away the surrounding trees, leaving their selection exposed to the elements so it becomes even stronger and more flexible.

In life, your main mast is made up of your most cherished values, the ones that won't fail you when the going gets rough. When your sails are set and the fierce winds of life begin to buffet you, your most cherished values remain strong yet resilient. They sustain and give you strength during difficult times.

A vision that's not aligned with your most cherished values will never make you happy. Bryan, a 60-year-old lawyer, values health, fun, financial independence, and his family. His first two values support his vision of retiring and playing golf all the time. However, if he's not careful to spend quality time with his family, and if he hasn't saved enough to support himself financially, his last two values won't be met and he won't be a happy man.

After 30 years with the same company, Mike was forced to retire when his firm was bought out. At age 56, he was neither mentally nor financially ready to retire, so he completed the process you're about to learn and identified his most cherished values. They included religion, helping others, teaching, and winning—an unusual combination, but one that suited him perfectly for a career in real estate. "I think the new job allows me to maintain and practice the values I have," Mike said. "It allows me the flexibility to be with my family and attend church. I like helping young people avoid mistakes when buying a house. I'm getting to teach to a certain extent, by helping new agents when they start out. Real estate involves negotiation, and I always like to win at negotiating." Identifying his values let Mike turn his unwanted retirement into an exciting and rewarding opportunity.

Here's a simple exercise to help you discover and prioritize your most cherished values. Don't be deceived by its apparent length—it won't take long to do, and it's well worth the effort.

The Values Process

If you're like most people, you'll probably identify with many of the values on the following list, and narrowing it down may seem daunting at first. That's why the process is done in three steps. Take your time, follow the instructions, and remember *there are no wrong answers.* This exercise is simply intended to help you identify your most cherished values.

Step 1: For each value, circle the number that best indicates its importance to you (1 = not important, 3 = important). Remember, you're ultimately going to narrow this list down to your top four, so be selective: Try to save the 3s for your 10 to 20 *most cherished* values. Use the "Other" spaces at the end to add values that are important to you but aren't on the list.

Value (description)	*Not important* ⇒ *Important*		
Acceptance (tolerance, openness, fairness)	1	2	3
Adventure (variety, challenge, excitement)	1	2	3
Aesthetics (beauty, grace, elegance)	1	2	3
Ambition (vision, goals, accomplishment)	1	2	3
Authenticity (naturalness, integrity, honesty)	1	2	3
Balance (steadiness, stability)	1	2	3
Compassion (forgiveness, encouragement, tactfulness)	1	2	3
Competition (winning, dominating, taking risks)	1	2	3
Conscientiousness (devotion, dedication, precision)	1	2	3
Contribution (service, volunteering, generosity)	1	2	3
Courage (strength, boldness, assertiveness)	1	2	3
Creativity (innovation, expression, flexibility)	1	2	3
Determination (focus, discipline, self-control)	1	2	3
Diligence (hard work, alertness, thoroughness)	1	2	3
Discernment (clear thinking, awareness, practicality)	1	2	3
Enthusiasm (zeal, dynamism, passion)	1	2	3

Value (description)	*Not important* ➠ *Important*		
Family happiness	1	2	3
Fun (pleasure, entertainment, playfulness)	1	2	3
Gratitude	1	2	3
Growth (advancement, improvement, self-actualization)	1	2	3
Happiness (joy, bliss, radiance)	1	2	3
Health & fitness (energy, youthfulness, attractiveness)	1	2	3
Humility (modesty)	1	2	3
Humor (wit, joviality)	1	2	3
Independence (self-reliance, freedom, autonomy)	1	2	3
Knowledge (discovery, wisdom, foresight)	1	2	3
Leadership (influence, power, authority)	1	2	3
Legacy (bequest, heritage, inheritance)	1	2	3
Love (intimacy, nurturing, connection)	1	2	3
Loyalty (duty, allegiance, fidelity)	1	2	3
Order (organization, stability, dependability)	1	2	3
Precision (meticulousness, preparation, punctuality)	1	2	3
Quality (excellence, professionalism, customer service)	1	2	3
Relationships (community, teamwork, affiliation)	1	2	3
Respect (pride, worth, confidence)	1	2	3
Responsibility (accountability, trustworthiness, reliability)	1	2	3
Spirituality (faith, optimism, balance, self-renewal)	1	2	3
Success (fame, rank, status)	1	2	3
Talent (skill, experience, expertise)	1	2	3
Tranquility (simplicity, gentleness, security)	1	2	3
Uniqueness (originality, specialness)	1	2	3
Wealth (financial freedom, economic security)	1	2	3
Other	1	2	3
Other	1	2	3

Step 2: Look at all the 3s you circled. If you have more than ten, place a check mark next to the ten that are *most important* to you, then write them in any order on the following lines. Using the same process you used in Step 1, circle the number that indicates each value's level of importance. Again, try to reserve the 5s for your *top four* values.

Value (description)	Important ➠ Very Important	
1.	4	5
2.	4	5
3.	4	5
4.	4	5
5.	4	5
6.	4	5
7.	4	5
8.	4	5
9.	4	5
10.	4	5

Step 3: From the 5s you circled in Step 2, select your top four values and write them on the following lines. You may find it helpful to write a sentence or two, clearly describing what each value means to you. You might want to use a dictionary, thesaurus, important wisdom literature, or scriptures to help you understand the deeper meaning of the words.

My Top 4 Values

1.

2.

3. _____

_____

4. _____

_____

Remember, your most cherished values are like a ship's main mast. Whether life is smooth sailing or full of storms, you can hold onto your values to guide your decisions. Assume you want to live the rest of your life honoring and fulfilling the values you've selected.

5. What Measurable, Achievable Goals Will You Set and What Actions Must You Take to Achieve Them?

Once your mast is firmly in place, you can raise the sails and use the rudder to guide your ship toward the treasure. Without a steering mechanism, you'd be blown all over the sea by the prevailing winds. Manning the rudder is a great metaphor for the hard work of steering yourself toward your goals. Remember, a vision pulls you into the future; goals push you toward your ultimate destination.

It's also important to plot on the map the actual time frame for reaching a certain destination. People often set goals too quickly. Take time to think about the measurable, achievable goals that will help you accomplish your vision. Then just do the next spontaneous right action, guided by your heart. Notice that your heart is intelligent and can guide you. It's your conscience, that deeper part of you that's wise. Choose to do the next right action, the next step, and your heart will be a guidance system within you.

Ed, a 71-year-old former vice president of marketing, retired several years ago—if you can call it that. Before retiring, Ed took some time to think about his vision, purpose, values, and beliefs. He made a list of his interests, abilities, and some activities he'd always wanted to do. He tried several items on the list and discovered new interests and passions. His visioning process led him to choose specific goals, such as serving on the advisory boards and boards of directors of three different companies; volunteering much of his time; and setting up a family foundation and scholarship fund. Now, every New Year's Day, Ed makes a new list of goals to accomplish in the coming year.

Most of my clients find it even more powerful to work with a coach who helps them set goals and be accountable for achieving them. If you're ready to go beyond writing New Year's resolutions on a piece of paper and start setting exciting, life-altering goals written in your heart, the following questions will get you started.

- What goals do you now have for living your vision of possibilities?
- What will you do to lead a rich life?
- What lasting legacy do you want to leave for others?
- Is what you're doing today moving you closer to or farther away from your compelling vision and most cherished values?

6. How Will You Celebrate the Treasures of Your Life?

Continuing our metaphor of being on a treasure hunt, imagine you've reached your goal and landed on shore. You do some hard work, some digging, and there it is—your treasure. You discover your heart's desire: Your true passion. Better relationships. Better management of your money. The trip of a lifetime. A mission to help people. Impact on your community. Enough money to pay your bills, and then more. Gratitude for life's simplest moments. Restored energy. Healed wounds. Reconciled relationships. A new career. Vitality when you wake up in the morning, and peace of mind as you lay your head on your pillow each night.

You've connected to your vision; articulated your purpose; and acknowledged old, inefficient patterns. You've prioritized your values and set specific goals. Now it's time to celebrate. With a newfound attitude of thanksgiving and celebration, no matter what happens, you'll have an inner experience of deep, abiding joy. Even if something awful happens, like a spouse dies, the work you've done will allow you to grieve and yet celebrate the life you lived together.

Carolyn had achieved much by her late 40s. She was a great mom who raised two sons and helped her husband start and run a very lucrative business. Under their joint leadership, the company was named by *Inc.* magazine as number 35 of the 500 fastest-growing companies. One day, to her great shock, Carolyn's husband asked for a divorce.

Although she had a lot of money in the bank, Carolyn didn't count it as her main treasure. Devastated by the divorce, she sought out counseling and coaching to uncover her assets beyond tangible dollars. "I found myself coming apart," she recalled. "I'd lost my husband. I lost my life, really. I went from being a wife and mother to having no identity of my own. In the last eleven years, I've taken the time to figure out who I am, what's important, and what I want out of this life."

Carolyn's hard work paid off in a big way. She'd taken the time to discover the big picture, clearly define her purpose, overcome old patterns, get her values in order, and set achievable goals. A few years later, when her greatest treasure—her health—was threatened by the diagnosis of breast cancer, Carolyn weathered the storm with commitment, vision, and courage.

"I was praying," she said, "and I would hear God say to me, 'It's just an inconvenience. It's just an inconvenience.' To me, 'It's just an inconvenience' meant 'You just have to do the tests and everything's going to be fine.' Then I got the results—cancer."

"It's just an inconvenience," she kept telling herself.

One day, when her hair was falling out from the chemotherapy, she received a visit from a neighbor's sister. The woman, a former nun, had gone through breast cancer a few years earlier and dropped by to offer encouragement and support. "We were sitting in the living room," Carolyn remembered, "and she said, 'Well, Carolyn, I just want you to look at this as just an inconvenience.'

And I said, 'I got the message!'"

"It's just an inconvenience" became a treasured saying for Carolyn as she found the spirit to face and win her battle with cancer.

As Carolyn's story demonstrates, the sixth guideline is about being able to celebrate during bad times as well as good. With a newfound attitude of "No regrets," nothing can stop you from celebrating life. No matter what tragedies may occur, you can celebrate the lessons you've learned and expand your happiness every day.

As you think about the answers to the following questions, focus your attention on the treasures in your life:

- What treasure comes with this goal that you really want to celebrate?

- How will you celebrate life richly?

- How have your troubles been your teachers?

- How would you now define happiness?

7. How Will You Use Your Treasure to Serve Others and Make a Difference?

Your treasure goes way beyond money. It also includes your talents, gifts, resources, and health. However, the greatest treasure of all is sharing your wealth through your service. This last guideline invites you to take your treasure into the world and offer it as a gift to others, by giving without regard to the fruits of your actions.

A young man was about to take over his father's long-established business. The father was well known for his success, both financially and in the intangible asset of having earned great community esteem. The father, offering his son some business advice, said, "Son, whenever you meet any customer or potential customer, always approach them this way." The father held his arm straight out, as if he were offering something. "Don't approach a customer in this manner," he continued, moving his arm as if he were grabbing or taking something away. "At work or at home, always give without regard to gain, and all of life's most important treasures will be at your disposal." The son never forgot his father's wise advice.

We spend so much time hunting, gathering, storing, and spending our treasures, but until we share them with others we have no real wealth. This final guideline challenges you to make a difference by sharing your treasures in the world. If you're willing to energetically serve others and let your newfound wealth flow freely, consider the answers to the following questions:

- How can you use your treasure to serve other people?

- What can you do with the money and resources you've found?

- What kind of lasting legacy do you want to leave for others?

- How will you use your wealth to create win-win transactions that benefit others as well as yourself?

The Power of a Vision

If you apply these seven visioning guidelines successfully, you'll produce a vivid picture of your future life. You'll be able to see, feel, smell, and almost touch your new goals. More important, you'll be able to formulate a plan to help you reach those goals.

Taking time to vision can lead you to a new internal motivation that will redirect your life's purpose. Visioning can help you re-create the inspired mind of the imaginative child you used to be. Use your life experiences—what you liked, what worked, what gave you pleasure and fulfillment—as the basis for envisioning a new purpose for your life after 50.

With a compelling vision, no dream is too big to accomplish. The vision supplies the motivation, and the motivation sweeps away any resistance, just as it did when you were young. Excuses like, "It's too late, I'm too busy, it will take too long" become minor roadblocks, easily removable. You'll experience once again the passionate pursuit of a life purpose that makes you feel truly alive. You'll restore and breathe new life into your present self-image.

Once you have the vision, it's a short step to formulating concrete goals. Once you have the goals, you can evaluate all your future actions. If the action is consistent with your goals, you'll take it, no matter what. If the action is inconsistent with your goals, you won't take it and you won't spend any time worrying about it.

One of the world's wealthiest individuals, Bill Gates, recently committed $24 billion of his personal wealth to the goal of providing health care for the world's poorest children. Before making that commitment, Bill Gates was merely a very wealthy man. After he made the commitment, he became a wealthy man who could make an enormous contribution to the world. The difference was not the wealth, but his vision of how to apply it to a bigger purpose. You may never have the financial resources of a Bill Gates, but you too can make a difference in the world—if you have a vision.

Making your vision come true will require two additional things: being in good physical condition and being in good financial condition. The next few chapters are about the physical side. Then we'll turn our attention to finances. However, before you leave this chapter, please take a moment to review the seven visioning guidelines for finding your life's treasure.

◆ ◆ ◆

Coaching Questions

What's Your Vision for Your Future Life?

1. What are the possibilities for your life?

2. What's your purpose?

3. What old, ineffective patterns could sabotage your treasure hunt?

4. Which of your most cherished values will sustain you on your treasure hunt?

5. What measurable, achievable goals will you set and what actions must you take to achieve them?

6. How will you celebrate the treasures of your life?

7. How will you use your treasure to serve others and make a difference?

Chapter 4

TRAIN TO ACHIEVE YOUR PHYSICAL BEST

D riving to work one morning, I noticed a tiny, gray-haired woman jogging along the side of the road. Although she was well built, dressed in workout gear, and zipping along at a pretty good pace, her gray hair and wrinkled face led me to believe she was at least 70, or maybe older. After a few weeks of seeing her daily in all kinds of weather, I was more than a little curious to find out who she was and why she ran.

It didn't take long to track her down. Everyone in town seemed to know Leona, not only from her running, but also through her community involvement. I quickly learned that she could be found three mornings a week at a nearby church—participating in an aerobics class. That's where I caught up with her, introducing myself as the class let out. I asked her for an interview and she cheerfully agreed, so we scheduled an appointment for later that afternoon. Then I got into my car and turned to wave good-bye. Instead of getting into a car of her own, there was Leona, jogging across the parking lot and heading down the street.

Arriving at her apartment later that day, I found it to be pretty much the way I expected. There were pictures of the grandkids and doilies on the tables. Comfortable-looking furniture was tastefully arranged. Then I spotted an exercise bike in front of the TV. A slant board in the hallway. Free weights and a "gut buster" under the coffee table.

In case you don't know what a gut buster is, it's a little wheel with handle grips where the axle normally goes. You get down on your knees, hold onto the handles, and roll forward as far as you can, then back. With Leona's encouragement, I got on the floor and gave it a try. I rolled out and back a few times, until Leona exclaimed, "Oh, Tom! Let me show you how to do it." Dropping to her knees, she quickly and efficiently did eight or nine reps. Then she got up and proudly displayed her very impressive biceps.

Leona didn't start running until age 54. "Before that time," she said, "you didn't hear that much about running. But it started to get popular and I thought, *I'd like to try that.* So I would walk to one lamppost and then run to the other, and keep that up. Then the next time run two, and that's the way I built up to it." And build she did. In 2002, at age 81, Leona ran her sixth consecutive annual half-marathon. She proudly informed me that her time had improved every single year. "You know, I surprised myself," she said. "At my age, you're not supposed to be faster, you're supposed to go downhill."

I asked Leona whether she considers herself a runner or a jogger. "I used to call myself a jogger, so a lot of people call me a jogger," she explained. "As I've been doing better, and more of it, I like people to say (and a lot of them do), 'Oh, are you the lady I see running?' And I say, 'Yeah.'" Leona personifies something runner and writer George Sheehan once said: "The difference between a jogger and a runner is an entry blank."

Before you conclude that running a half-marathon is no big deal, let me tell you a little more about the event in which Leona participates. The Indianapolis Life 500 Festival Mini-Marathon is a 13.1-mile tour of downtown Indianapolis, with a lap around the Indianapolis Motor Speedway, home of the Indianapolis 500, Brickyard 400, and U.S. Grand Prix. It's one of our nation's largest half-marathons, with more than 19,500 racers crossing the finish line in 2004. While you might expect half-marathoners to be young people, 14 percent of that year's participants were 50 years old or older, and 62 of them (48 men and 14 women) ran in the

70-and-up divisions. In 2002, Leona took first place among women 75 and older, finishing the race in 3 hours, 10 minutes, and coming out ahead of nearly 4,500 other runners—many of them decades younger than herself.

Now, I'm not suggesting that you drop everything and become a long-distance runner. I simply offer Leona as a role model of possibilities, and I hope her achievements inspire you as much as they did me. When I think about her training routine— running a mile and a half to and from aerobics class three days a week and a scenic seven-mile route the other four days, doing sit-ups on her slant board, pedaling her exercise bike, lifting weights, and walking most afternoons—what possible excuse does some-one my age have for failing to accomplish my fitness goals? Leona is a shining example for anyone who wants to enjoy an active lifestyle. And when I remind myself that she didn't start running until her mid 50s, I can't help but realize it's never too late for any of us to start training for healthy longevity.

Why Exercise?

"We are our choices."
—Jean-Paul Sartre, French philosopher

Whether you consider yourself adventuresome or tame, whether you want to run half-marathons or take a relaxing ocean voyage, you'll enjoy the activities a lot more if you're in the best shape you can possibly be. You probably don't need me to tell you this, but no matter how old or young you are, setting specific fit-ness goals and training to achieve them will enhance every area of your life.

Countless books, studies, and governmental reports confirm that exercising regularly is one of the best things you can do to improve your overall fitness. In the 1996 *Report on Physical Activity and Health* (USA, 1996), the U.S. Surgeon General wrote, "Significant health benefits can be obtained with a moderate amount of physical activity, preferably daily." According to the National Center of Physical Activity and Disability, those benefits include:

- Increased cardiac (heart) and pulmonary (lung) function
- Improved ability to perform activities of daily living
- Protection against development of chronic diseases
- Decreased anxiety and depression
- Enhanced feeling of well-being
- Weight control
- Lowered cholesterol and blood pressure

Dr. Ralph Paffenbarger, an authority on the epidemiology of chronic diseases and a professor emeritus at Stanford University School of Medicine, studied more than 71,000 alumni from the University of Pennsylvania and Harvard College. His College Alumni Health Study, under way since 1960, focuses on individuals who graduated between 1916 and 1950 (men and women born between 1896 and 1934). In the *American Journal of Epidemiology* (Feb. 2000), Dr. Paffenbarger and I. M. Lee concluded that their data "showed that vigorous activity . . . clearly predicted lower mortality rates."

Dr. Paffenbarger is also widely recognized for his pioneering studies of San Francisco longshoremen. He found a significantly lower risk of heart attack among hardworking cargo handlers than among the less active walking bosses and warehousemen. Paffenbarger's studies demonstrated the protective effects of vigorous exercise.

I could spend the rest of this chapter citing studies and listing statistics about why you should exercise, but I think you get the point. You *know* exercise is good for you—it can help you live longer, reduce health risks, and generally make you feel better. Yet, if you're like most people, you probably don't do it. Despite the obvious benefits, only three out of ten Americans exercise regularly (U.S. Health and Human Services Secretary Tommy Thompson, 2002).

Have you ever begun an exercise program, only to stop it a few weeks later? Have you ever made a New Year's resolution to take up jogging or join a gym, then forgotten all about it by Valentine's Day? Maybe you're one of the few who exercises regularly, but you've hit a plateau and need to push a little harder to reach the next level. Or maybe you're one of those really rare people who's made a lifetime commitment to physical health. Wherever you are in terms of your fitness, you'll have even more success in achieving your goals by developing a training mentality for life.

Develop a Training Mentality

You're probably familiar with the old adage, I wish I'd known then what I know now. It implies that by the time you figure things out, it's too late to do you any good. Your only recourse is to leave a legacy of wisdom to the generation behind you, and hope they'll use it before it's too late.

The previous generation left a legacy for us, though I'm sure it was unintentional. Not expecting to live so long, they were unprepared for longevity. As a result, many of them spent their later years physically unable to do what they wanted.

Luckily, we have an alternative. We can learn from their example and do something different. We can create the possibility of feeling like we're 50 well into our 70s, 80s, and beyond. We can take steps now to stay healthy, fit, and active for many years to come. We can choose to believe that as we get older, we'll have the potential to be at our peak in performance and productivity. However, achieving peak performance later in life requires us to do something no previous generation has ever done before— train for our longevity.

Let's consider for a moment this concept of training and how it differs from exercise. World-class athletes don't just exercise, they train for their success. They discipline themselves to think healthy thoughts, eat properly, maintain their physical health, shape optimistic attitudes, and develop hidden potential. Exercise is beneficial; when you exercise, you feel vitalized. But training involves the ongoing practice of disciplines that help you achieve and maintain a performance state for extended periods of time. It requires a synergy of mental, physical, and emotional variables.

If you're just exercising, you can accept less than full effort in your program. After all, you showed up, right? If you're in training, anything less than your best keeps you from attaining the change and improvement you seek.

If you're just exercising, you can skip a workout or two, and it won't bother you at all. If you're in training, missing a workout sets you back from where you could have been in terms of improved strength, flexibility, and endurance.

If you're just exercising, it's okay to skip the occasional meal or indulge in that sugary snack you crave. If you're in training, you know you need good nutrition to support your efforts in the gym, on the practice range, and on the course. Anything less than your ideal eating plan sabotages the work you've done.

In the same way, adopting a training mentality for longevity can help you make life after 50 your best years yet. Creating a training mentality is as easy as flipping a switch. You simply *decide* that you're in training for a long and healthy life. That's it. From that point forward, everything you do from an exercise perspective suddenly becomes more purposeful. With a training mentality, it becomes easy to prioritize and make small sacrifices to achieve your goals.

Now, to take this concept one giant step further, let's apply the seven keys to this area of life and create total physical abundance.

Key #1: Take Time to Create a Compelling Vision

Before you'll take action in any area of life, you need your own reasons to get you started. That's where key #1 comes in—

when you develop an exciting vision of your physical condition, you'll feel compelled to take actions in the present to make that vision come true. When it comes to exercising, key #1 is about envisioning a stronger, healthier you.

Before you even consider beginning or changing your exercise program, take time to think about what you hope to be, do, or accomplish. What end result do you want to obtain? How do you want to look 5, 10, or 20 years from now? What do you want to be able to do physically? How do you want to feel?

The following exercise can jump-start your thinking and help you create a compelling vision. You can read it through and just keep going, or take a few minutes to turn on some music and jot down some notes as you think about your future.

- *Let your mind go wild!* See yourself being in the best possible shape you could be at 60, 75, or 100 years old. What would you look like? What could you do? How long do you think you'd live if you were in your ultimate physical condition? Would you wear a smaller belt or dress size? Play a better round of golf, or maybe shoot your age? Bench-press 200 pounds? Run a five-minute mile or a three-and-a-half-hour marathon? Rock and roll at your grandchild's wedding? Bend over and pick up your great-grandchildren at 80, 90, or 100 years old without straining your back or breaking a hip?

  Think about what you'd like to accomplish in terms of your physical condition, and form a picture in your mind. Don't impose limits by telling yourself it can't be done. Don't worry about how you'll make your dreams come true; we'll get to that part later. For now, just let your mind run loose and enjoy the possibilities.

- *Involve all five senses.* The more senses you can involve in your visualization, the more real the picture will be and the stronger your drive will become.

If you envision yourself dancing at your grandchild's wedding, *see* yourself dancing in the beautifully decorated room. *Feel* that special someone in your arms as you move in time with the music. *Hear* the other guests talking about how great you look. *Smell* the flowers that decorate the room, and *taste* that first sip of champagne as you toast the bride and groom.

Maybe you'd rather bench-press 200 pounds. *See* yourself lying on the bench, getting ready to raise the barbell. *Feel* the cold metal bar as you grip it with both hands. *Smell* the musky odor of the gym, *taste* the sweat in your mouth, and *hear* your breath as you inhale and exhale deeply. How would you feel if you could lift that amount? How would your body look? What else would you be able to do?

- *Practice, practice, practice.* Strong mental pictures can lead to better results. Once you've identified a compelling vision for your physical condition, come back to it often. See yourself dancing at the wedding, lifting the weight, taking the perfect golf swing, or crossing the finish line at the end of the race. When you practice the results enough times in your mind, taking the intermediate steps to achieve them becomes easy and automatic.

A Record-Breaking Vision

Until 1954, medical experts were certain that no human being could run a mile in less than four minutes. When Roger Bannister did it, he broke a psychological barrier as well as a physical one. Once he cleared the way, everyone knew it could be done—his record was broken within two months.

Key #2: Connect Your Vision to Your Values, Passion, and Purpose

When you tie your fitness vision to your most cherished values, exercising can take on a higher meaning and become part of a greater purpose. Leona, the runner you met at the beginning of this chapter, produced powerful results by creating a compelling vision for her physical condition and connecting it with some of her deepest values. In her 50s, she imagined seeing herself looking good and feeling healthy for many years to come. Since her values included being outdoors and having a social network, she used racing and aerobics classes to achieve her vision while simultaneously meeting those values.

Leona also admitted that she enjoys the recognition she gets in the process: "I really think I like the attention," she confessed. "When I do the Mini, when I come in, they announce my name: 'Here's Leona!' All these good runners, yelling and screaming and clapping. I love that!" Leona doesn't have to wait all year to meet her values of recognition and social contact. She meets them on a daily basis, by stopping to chat with friends, neighbors, and curious strangers who marvel at her energy and athletic ability.

Gail, a 60-something retired schoolteacher, lists rewarding relationships among her most cherished values. Her husband died several years ago, and her son's family lives far away, so she's had to create a new "family." By combining her values with her exercise plan, she found a way to meet people, surround herself with a continually expanding group of friends, and stay in great shape, all at the same time. Gail plays tennis in three different leagues, setting goals for herself to win championships. She's the oldest player by five years in her over-50 group, but she usually wins because of the skills she perfects while playing with the "younger girls" (the 35-year-olds). By combining her values and fitness goals, she's made friends of all ages and enjoys their company both on and off the tennis courts.

Frank and Betty Ann, a couple in their early 80s, share a value of traveling to exotic locales. Being in good shape is important to them—they have sights to see, luggage to carry, and trains and planes to board. Their spirituality is also an important value, and they participate in a number of church activities. They've found a way to combine both of these values with their fitness routine. Since their church is near their home, they stay in shape by riding their bikes to committee meetings, socials, and other church events. By tying their fitness vision to their most cherished values, they get plenty of exercise while doing things they anticipate and enjoy.

Have you ever noticed that you'll always find time for the things you value most? Training is no different. To turn your fitness program into a fun, exciting, rewarding activity that you'll look forward to doing on a regular basis, try tapping into the vision, values, purpose, and passion you identified in chapter 3. Here are a few ideas to consider:

- *If you value spending time with family and friends,* ask them to join you for a walk, a bike ride, or a run through the park. Invite them to take advantage of a two-for-one membership at the gym with you. Set goals together to compete in a race or participate in an event that would require you to train beyond your current level.

- *If you're passionate about your spiritual side,* use your exercise time to pray or draw closer to whatever higher power you believe in. Set a goal to participate in an event sponsored by a cause you support.

- *If your purpose in life is to teach others,* take classes to become a coach, teacher, or trainer of some sort. Learn to teach children to dance or become an instructor at your local fitness center. Again, set a goal for yourself in this area that takes you beyond your comfort zone.

What do you value most? What are you absolutely passionate about in life? When you connect your training program to your values, vision, purpose, and passion, the time you spend working out will fly by, and you'll find yourself wishing it didn't have to end.

So, what are you waiting for? Consider your vision, values, passion, and purpose; envision the fitness level you want to achieve; and come up with fun ways to tie them together. Let your imagination run wild. The possibilities are endless, and the rewards will be unlimited.

Key #3: Educate Yourself and Find a Great Coach

When it comes to physical conditioning, you'll find a wide variety of activities from which to choose. There's aerobic exercise, strength training, bodybuilding, and Jazzercise. There's Taebo, tai chi, kickboxing, and Pilates. Weightlifting, water aerobics, hiking, biking, and rollerblading. How can you possibly know which is best for you?

Fortunately, there are plenty of resources available for someone seeking an education. You'll find some of them listed in the Recommended Reading list at the end of this book. However, one of the best ways to learn about fitness is to work with a coach or personal trainer.

For the last three years, I've trained with Bill Hartman, an outstanding personal trainer and a licensed physical therapist. Bill earned his degree in movement and sports science from Purdue University. He's a Certified Strength and Conditioning Specialist by the National Strength and Conditioning Association, as well as a USA Weightlifting Sport Performance Coach. I called upon Bill for help with this chapter, and he provided much of the information you're about to learn.

Personal Training: Is It for You?

No one should start a training program without some guidance from a professional. Although you could design a program for yourself, if you go wrong, you're likely to become frustrated, quit, or even injure yourself.

There are three main reasons to hire a personal trainer:

1. A trainer provides an organized system for attaining the goals that made you start exercising in the first place.

2. Working with a trainer can help you significantly lessen your chances of hurting yourself as you exercise.

3. A trainer makes the process of getting fit more efficient. You'll save a lot of time and get better results if you seek professional help from the outset.

Finding a qualified trainer can be a daunting task. Personal recommendations are a good place to start, but the people you ask may desire different results than you do, and their "wonderful" trainer might not be appropriate for you. For example, a trainer recommended by long-distance runners may not be a good choice for you if you're not interested in long-distance running.

Credentials are important, but they shouldn't be your only guideline. Contrary to popular belief, "certification" doesn't qualify an individual as a quality personal trainer. There are no standards for or regulation of certified personal training, and many poorly qualified, poorly trained people may have purchased their certification from a company that does nothing but certify trainers. I find it amazing that you'd have to be licensed by the state in which you lived before you could cut someone's hair, but anyone can call themselves a personal trainer or fitness expert.

Ideally, a trainer should have both a medical and an exercise background. For example, someone who has worked as a physical therapist would know how to conduct an orthopedic assessment. He or she would also be sensitive to spinal and other potential problems.

Some trainers tend to train people like they train themselves, rather than creating an individualized program. George, the 67-year-old anesthesiologist you met in chapter 2, tried working with one such trainer and quickly became discouraged. "A lot of the trainers are just used to working with younger people," he observed. "They're great for pushing weight to the max. At my age, I'm not interested in developing much. It's kind of hard for these young trainers to realize that."

If someone offers a cookie-cutter approach—one they say

applies to you and all exercisers—you may find yourself in an unsafe program. Bill has witnessed instances of seeing people in gyms who "look like heart attacks waiting to happen, while their trainer stands over them and screams at them to lift a weight they shouldn't even attempt. A trainer who can't recognize people at cardiovascular risk shouldn't be training anyone," he warns.

Approaches like the ones George and Bill describe are based on a lack of knowledge and experience. Look for someone who offers each client a personalized training program and knows how to work with people your age.

Interview Questions for Effective Screening

Since there are no standards of education for personal trainers, it's imperative that you test a trainer before hiring him or her. Remember, the first step is to educate yourself so you can ask intelligent questions. Learn about exercise in general, the amount of effort it may take to reach your goal, and the specific types of exercise you're considering (you'll find some basics later in this chapter).

After you've armed yourself with a good education, call several trainers and schedule interviews with each. The following questions should help you assess their qualifications. They cover the person's background, experience, and basic knowledge of exercise physiology.

Questions to Discover a Trainer's Basic Background

1. **Do you have a college degree in an exercise-related field?** A degree indicates trainers who've been exposed to a wealth of information about exercise and fitness. It means they didn't just study for 30 days, pass one test, and call themselves trainers.

2. **How long have you been a personal trainer?** Experience counts—sometimes. Being a long-time trainer does not guarantee significant experience; some trainers work only a few hours a week. On the other hand, a relatively

inexperienced trainer who studied under a well-educated or highly regarded trainer, and has been immersed in the latest training information, may provide a higher quality of service than someone who's been a trainer for years.

3. ***Are you certified? By which organization?*** At the time of this printing, the American College of Sports Medicine (ACSM) and the National Strength and Conditioning Association (NSCA) are considered the "gold standards" of certifying organizations. They require candidates to have a college degree (or be currently enrolled in the last term of a degree program) in a health-related field before taking their exams. At the opposite end of the spectrum are the companies that provide general exercise-related information and an exam for a price. In essence, they "sell" certification. To say such certification is nationally or internationally recognized means nothing, since there are no uniform standards established for such recognition.

4. ***Can I get regular appointments that fit my schedule? How do you expect to be paid? What happens if either of us misses an appointment?*** There are no right or wrong answers here, but the trainer should have established policies and you should be comfortable with them. At the time of this printing, trainers charge anywhere from $15 to $200 per session. Depending on where you live, a reasonable amount to invest is about $30 to $75 per session.

5. ***Can you treat minor injuries if they occur?*** Any trainer should be able to treat injuries with RICE (rest, ice, compression, and elevation) and then refer you to a physician for further treatment.

6. ***Do you know CPR and have proof of your CPR training?*** Although this is a worst-case scenario, if you suffer a heart attack in the trainer's presence, he or she should be able to administer CPR until help arrives.

You may not want to ask all the questions I've listed. In that case, just pick the ones you feel comfortable using. If potential trainers are insulted by your questioning, they're probably not the right trainers for you. Even worse, if they can't answer your questions, keep looking until you find someone who can.

Key #4: Formulate and Implement a Measurable Plan

The first step in devising an effective plan is to set measurable, attainable intermediate goals. Exercise for the sake of exercise isn't much fun, but training to achieve a specific goal is. Leona, the octogenarian you met earlier in this chapter, probably wouldn't run every day just for the heck of it. She runs because she keeps her sights set on her vision of looking and feeling great, and on her specific goal of running in the next Mini-Marathon. George, the anesthesiologist I mentioned earlier, started exercising to reduce his high blood pressure. He knew losing weight could help.

What specific goals would you like to achieve? Do you want to lose weight? Tighten your belt? Lower your blood pressure or cholesterol levels? Be able to run several miles without stopping? Consider a boxing comeback, like 55-year-old George Foreman? Climb Mt. Everest on your 60th birthday? Run half-marathons in your 70s and 80s like Leona? Parachute from an airplane the day you turn 80, like former president George Bush? (He's already announced plans to do it again at age 90.)

Before you read any further, take a minute or two to think about an exciting or compelling goal you want to achieve, something that would give you a target to shoot for on your way to healthy longevity.

Before You Get Started

The information in this book is not intended to take the place of medical or personal training advice. Strenuous exercise has risks that you should discuss with your physician. The American Heart Association recommends that if you're over 45 and have not had a physical exam in two years or longer; or if you have serious or chronic medical conditions or are at risk for heart disease; or if you're on medication, you should consult a physician before embarking on a serious exercise program. A professional assessment of your physical condition can also provide an accurate starting point from which to measure your progress and alert you to any problems or conditions that require special attention.

Tell your physician you want to start an exercise program and you're concerned about strength, flexibility, and aerobic conditioning. Even if the physician is not an expert on exercise, he or she can still perform tests (such as treadmill tests) to evaluate you for health risks, cardiovascular condition, and other medical concerns. If the tests uncover a heart problem, for example, you'll need to work with your doctor to design a training program that will not overly tax your heart.

Your physician may refer you to a physical therapist for an assessment of posture, range of motion, and any potential skeletal problems. Anyone with orthopedic problems should undergo a whole-body assessment before starting a strength-training program. Unfortunately, the cost of such an assessment is not usually covered by health insurance, but the information you'll receive is worth the expense.

Choose an Appropriate Program

Armed with knowledge about your current condition, the next step is to educate yourself about exercise in general. First, it helps to be familiar with the overall components of physical fitness. These include:

- *Aerobic fitness,* which determines your ability to perform submaximal exercise for an extended period of time. Aerobic fitness has been associated with reduced risk of chronic diseases.

- *Muscle strength and endurance,* which determine how much weight you can lift and how long you can hold it.

- *Flexibility,* which determines your range of motion and reduces your risk of injury.

Next, you need some general knowledge about the type of exercise you're considering (such as aerobic versus anaerobic) and the amount of effort it will take to reach your goal. Suppose you wanted to lose 40 pounds in six months, and you decided to do it by walking a mile a day. Unless you knew that running or walking burns about 100 calories per mile and that you'd need to burn 3,500 calories to lose one pound, you'd probably embark upon your plan and be very disappointed when it didn't work out. With your plan, you'd lose only about a fifth of a pound per week, for a total of five to six pounds in a six-month period. At that rate, it would take almost four years to reach your goal of losing 40 pounds. Likewise, if you knew that weight training only burns about 200 to 300 calories per session, you could use that knowledge to determine an appropriate goal and design a plan to achieve it.

There are plenty of resources on exercise (see the Recommended Reading list at the end of this book), but here's some basic information to get you started.

Aerobic exercise typically refers to continuous, cyclical-type activities like running, biking, swimming, walking, and jogging. Aerobic exercise has been promoted in professional and popular exercise literature for years, mainly because:

- Its effects (increases in the heart's ability to pump blood) are easy to measure

- It encourages you to use your muscles

- It counteracts age-related decreases in the levels of fat-mobilizing enzymes, which can help you burn unwanted fat

- It leaves you feeling better psychologically

Aerobic fitness is important, but *strength training* is equally important. You can't walk on the beach, climb a hill, or carry a grandchild if you aren't strong enough to stand up in the first place. In his book, *Quantum Strength Fitness II* (Patrick's Books, 2000), Dr. Patrick O'Shea writes that starting at age 30, if you're not a regular strength trainer, you'll lose 6 to10 percent of your strength each decade. O'Shea, a professor emeritus in the Department of Exercise and Sports Science at Oregon State University, Corvallis, and a member of the USA Weightlifting Hall of Fame, goes on to explain that without strength training, you'll lose as much as 12 percent of your muscle mass by age 65. Strength is the difference between living your dreams and watching them pass you by.

Progressive strength training (working with weights) optimizes body function and helps keep you active. Health authorities now recommend that you perform at least moderate, regular (once or twice a week) training of every muscle group in the body.

Working as a physical therapist in a nursing home, Bill Hartman noticed that most of the elderly people there lacked agility, balance, strength, and proprioception (a sense of where the body is in space). He concluded that, for the aged, lack of strength, rather than cardiovascular fitness or capacity, was the limiting factor in their level of activity and ability to function. "In other words," he said, "if they don't have the strength to get out of a chair, take care of themselves, or maintain their balance, it doesn't really matter how strong their hearts are."

Strength training offers the following additional benefits:

- A potential decrease in the risk of injury due to stronger bones, muscles, and connective tissues
- A decreased risk of osteoporosis
- Better posture in your other daily activities

- An offset in the typical loss of muscle mass associated with aging

- Increased muscle mass and decreased chance of weight gain

- Reduced likelihood of loss of balance and falls

- Increased antioxidant production, which helps eliminate the tissue-damaging free radicals associated with accelerating the aging process

- Variety and flexibility in your exercise program

- Independence: Increased strength prevents a decline in function associated with aging, which means you can pursue your interests and maintain your active lifestyle

There's nothing wrong with using an exercise machine once in a while, as long as it allows you to progress toward your goals. However, using an exercise machine does not guarantee that you'll accomplish your goals or get balanced development of muscle groups. Most machines restrict your range of motion to a prescribed plane of movement, whereas free weights allow free movement along the joint's full range of motion. In the long run, you're much better off doing resistance training with free weights than with exercise machines.

There is one potential drawback to strength training: If you do it without proper guidance, you're likely to increase wear and tear on your joints. Some strength training techniques work for everybody, but you'll need professional guidance to learn what those are. *Never* start a strength training program without a proper medical evaluation and professional guidance from an experienced trainer. It's not appropriate to be self-directed in the beginning; it would be like performing surgery on yourself.

Flexibility training refers to stretching and strengthening exercises that improve joint range of motion and mobility. These exercises remove waste products that have aggregated during intense aerobic or strength training exercise. They also contribute to improved flexibility, which can enhance your performance in sports that require full joint motion, such as golf and tennis.

The Perfect Combination

Since no definitive scientific study proves that any one type of exercise is the "best" for staying healthy, you'll achieve maximum results by combining moderate levels of aerobic exercise with a program of progressive strength training and stretching, customized to meet your needs.

What blend of aerobic, strength, and flexibility training is optimal for you? It depends on your goals and how much time you're willing to spend. None of the three areas should be neglected. Look at your longevity training goals and choose the combination of exercises that will allow you to achieve them.

For example, if you're training to be better at a sport, take time to evaluate its metabolic needs and tailor your exercise program accordingly. A typical tennis match requires a lot of stop-and-go activity for up to five hours. Such a sport requires strong aerobic fitness, which can best be developed using aerobic activity and/or interval training. Conversely, a sport like golf requires you to be stationary for long periods of time (if you're riding in a cart), then take an aggressive swing. Those activities require a lot of power and flexibility, with less emphasis on aerobic fitness. If you want to climb mountains, a 50/50 blend of strength and aerobic training will help you build the strength you need for climbing and the aerobic capacity to efficiently utilize the decreased oxygen that exists at higher altitudes. If you're a competitive race-walker, the vast majority of your training should be aerobic, but you'll still want strength training to improve your balance, increase your ability to stand the stresses of the race, and become more stable so your gait is more efficient.

Again, there's no substitute for sound professional advice. Before setting your goals and implementing your plan, always seek medical clearance and professional instruction. Then work with your coach to follow through on a program of attainable intermediate goals.

Key #5: Monitor Your Progress and Update the Plan as Needed

I hope you noticed the word *attainable* at the end of that last sentence. Unless you choose attainable goals, you're setting yourself up to fail. Make attainability your litmus test, and you'll automatically set yourself up to win.

A few years ago, I decided to use the seven keys to tap into my life vision; connect it to my values, purpose, and passion; and create a fitness goal I could accomplish in honor of my 50th birthday. I decided to celebrate the big day by having a fun-filled triathlon with my good friends, Paul and his wife Pat. I envisioned myself playing a set of tennis, following it up with 36 holes of golf, then finishing the day by bench-pressing my weight (185 pounds).

If you examine my plan a little more closely, you'll see how I set myself up to win. My overall goal was to *celebrate my birthday by having a fun-filled triathlon with my good friends.* Even if I failed to complete one or more event, I could still have fun, be with my friends, and celebrate my birthday. In other words, I couldn't lose! By setting yourself up to win, no matter what you do, you can always be sure of finding fun in the journey and enjoying success along the way.

Getting back to the birthday story, I have to tell you I didn't succeed at every event. My tennis partner and I won the match, giving me bragging rights over Pat forever. (My partner, a strong player, carried more than her share of the weight, but that won't stop me from gloating about our victory.) Unfortunately, I'd envisioned myself playing on a clear, crisp morning; I neglected to factor in the heat and humidity for that time of year. In my enthusiasm, I spent about half an hour "warming up" at full strength. By the time we actually got going, the tennis match left me pretty drained. As a result, I only played 18 holes of golf and bench-pressed 175 pounds—10 pounds short of my goal but 40 pounds more than I could lift when I started training.

You probably think I was pretty disappointed, but I wasn't—not in the least. Why? Because I remembered key #5: Monitor your progress and update the plan as needed.

Visions and plans can and should be evaluated and revised on a regular basis. Right after my birthday, I identified my mistakes and redefined my goal. By incorporating the lessons I learned during my first attempt, I accomplished my triathlon later that year when the weather cooled off. I was still 50 when I completed the events and I had just as much fun the second time around, so I came out an even bigger winner.

It's important to keep key #5 in mind when you begin or intensify any exercise program. At first, you'll typically see some improvement; this is true of both aerobic and strength training exercise. However, your body eventually adapts to that level and becomes more efficient at performing it. Once your body adapts, you'll no longer see or feel the same rate of progress. That's when it's time to update your plan.

To get further benefit from aerobic exercise, you must increase your intensity by exercising at a higher percentage of your maximum heart rate. For example, if you chose walking as your form of exercise, you could increase your intensity by walking faster or walking uphill. Many people don't understand that aerobic exercise is an ongoing process of adaptation and change in stimulus; variables must continually be manipulated to promote gains.

The same is true of strength training: To be effective, it must be progressive. As your body gets used to an exercise, you must periodically increase the number of repetitions per set or the amount of weight you lift. If you're like most people, you'll get the maximum benefit of an exercise by performing it to the point of temporary muscle fatigue; if you can lift the weight more than 15 repetitions, then the weight is too light. If you can't lift it at least 6 times, the weight is too heavy. Try to stay within this range, and remember, if you fatigue closer to 6 repetitions, you're building muscle strength; if you fatigue closer to 15 repetitions, you're building muscle endurance. Your fitness goals should determine how many repetitions you do per set. In the beginning, you might only perform one set (that is, the number of repetitions followed by a period of rest) per exercise. As your body begins to adapt to the stress of strength training, you may choose to add more sets to your routine.

Hitting a plateau isn't the only time to revise or update your plan. Sometimes you need to try different strategies before you find one that works. George, the anesthesiologist you met earlier in this chapter, discovered his high blood pressure as the result of an insurance physical. His doctor prescribed medications, but George knew he should also lose weight. "I started walking right after I had the insurance exam," he said, "and actually began to see some results. But I had an old back injury, so swinging my arms and walking bothered my back. I've always enjoyed swimming, so I joined a health club where they had a pool. I started swimming every morning, then I started lifting weights and using the treadmill in the afternoons, holding onto the bars so I didn't have all that rotation and movement." Through trial and error, and an unwillingness to give up, George discovered the right combination for him. He's lost 35 pounds and his blood pressure is significantly lower.

Key #6: Enjoy Your Abundance

"What a disgrace it is for a man to grow old without ever seeing the beauty and strength of which his body is capable."
—Socrates, Greek philosopher

I'm sure you've heard the old expression, If you don't have your health, you don't have anything. Health and physical fitness are among the greatest gifts you can ever hope to attain. Key #6 is about pausing to enjoy and appreciate the gift of physical abundance.

Sometimes that abundance comes in unexpected ways. George intended to reduce his blood pressure and lose weight, but he also received an added surprise. After swimming, weightlifting, and walking on the treadmill for some time, he noticed one day that his back had stopped hurting. "It's all gone," he realized. "I never have any muscle problems in my neck anymore, I never have any problems with my back anymore. I can occasionally feel that the injury is still there, but I can go out and walk a mile or more and never have problems with my back." George not only noticed the difference—he celebrates his fitness with joy.

At 61 years old, Phyd and Dale enjoy the abundance they've created in their lives. In the last six years—meaning age 55 and over—they've hiked the Himalayas, gone on safari in Botswana, trekked through the Andes to Machu Pichu, sailed off the East Coast, and gone night diving in Curacao (where they turned off their lights and swam to shore 30 feet below the surface). At age 59, Dale went helicopter skiing five times in one day. Phyd, a power walker, finished several half-marathons before tackling the 26.2-mile Suzuki Rock and Roll Marathon in San Diego, California. As a participant in that event, she raised more money for charity than anyone else in the state of Indiana. Together, the couple climbed Mt. Kilimanjaro. Phyd trained for the event by power walking two hours a day; they both bicycled in their packs and boots and repeatedly ran the football stadium stairs—up, down, and backward.

Can you guess some of the values Phyd and Dale consider important? Their list includes travel, adventure, relationships, and contribution. By setting goals that meet their values, they've given themselves more than just a compelling reason to exercise and stay in shape. They're enjoying an abundance of physical fitness and healthy longevity.

Think for a moment about your training goals. Have you set yourself up to win by choosing attainable goals? Does your plan include ways for you to enjoy your abundance along the way, instead of at the end when you lose a certain number of pounds or fit into a particular outfit? Key #6 is a crucial part of training for healthy longevity. When you take time to enjoy your abundance every step of the way, you'll feel successful every day.

Key #7: Leave a Lasting Legacy

Phyd and Dale aren't the only ones who benefit from their abundance. They're also leaving a lasting legacy for their family, friends, and total strangers. Their children learn from their inspiring example. So do friends and neighbors who see this energetic couple walking, running, and biking through the community. And countless others gain from the fundraising and contributions that go along with many of the activities Dale and Phyd choose.

As you contemplate ways to make life after 50 your best years yet, how can you turn your training routine into a lasting legacy? Who could you invite to join you? Who might learn from your example? Which charities or worthwhile causes could benefit from your active participation?

Before you turn the page and leave this chapter, take a moment to contemplate the coaching questions that follow. With a strong training mentality and attainable goals, life after 50 can be your best years yet.

◆ ◆ ◆

Coaching Questions

Are You Training for Healthy Longevity?

- A strong, healthy lifestyle begins with a vision.

  How do you see yourself physically in your life after 50? What do you want to be, do, and have?

- Some people think it costs too much to exercise; they forget the cost of missed opportunities.

  What will it cost if you DON'T train for longevity? What will you miss out on? What price will you pay for letting yourself go?

- Remember, every journey begins with a single step.

  What one step could you take RIGHT NOW to begin or intensify your training routine? Do you need to interview a trainer, join a gym, or purchase a piece of exercise equipment? What single thing could you do today to start your training routine?

Chapter 5
NOURISH YOUR BODY FOR LIFELONG VITALITY

Have you ever gone to the gym, performed a great workout, and then followed it up with a quick trip to the nearest fast-food drive-through window? I hope the last chapter convinced you of the importance of regular exercise, but working out without watching what you eat is like having your car detailed and then filling the gas tank with lighter fluid. The car might look great on the outside, but it won't run smoothly or get you where you want to go.

Tom, a 55-year-old marketing executive, discovered the truth of this concept not long ago. He's one of those people who exercised twice a week but never paid much attention to his diet. He was a little overweight, but not big enough to do anything about it. Then, "I had a checkup and my cholesterol was high," he explained. "It was about 240. I could have gone on medication, but I thought, *Well, that's a marker. That could be telling me something.* So I decided to figure out how to get my cholesterol down. That was the motivating event."

Tom didn't know much about cholesterol, so he wisely contacted a registered dietitian—my wife, Kim Hardin—and asked her for advice. As the Indiana Dietetic Association's Young Dietitian of the Year in 1995; a frequent speaker at Indiana state conferences and local news broadcasts; and an experienced practitioner in clinical, marketing, and private settings, Kim was more than qualified to coach Tom in this area. In fact, she provided much of the information you'll find in this chapter.

"I always associated cholesterol with red meat," Tom recalled, "so I had to learn some other things about it. It's cheese, it's diet, and it's weight related, which I'd never understood. I've never seen anybody who's been on a diet, lost weight, and didn't gain it all back again, so I knew diets weren't going to work. That's when I talked to Kim and started to modify my behavior."

By following the plan they outlined together, Tom easily achieved his goals. Ten months later, his cholesterol is down to 201, his blood pressure (which had been borderline high) is 110/70, and he's lost about 30 pounds. He's thrilled with the way he looks and feels, and his success even benefited someone else: All his clothes had to be taken in twice, making his tailor, Karl, extremely happy.

By now, you're probably familiar enough with the seven keys to recognize them in Tom's story. Did you notice how he used them to solve his potentially life-threatening problem? Let's take a closer look at exactly what he did.

Key #1: Take Time to Create a Compelling Vision

> *"Eating well gives a spectacular joy to life and contributes immensely to goodwill."*
> —Elsa Schiaparelli, 19th-century fashion designer

As you read Tom's story, did you find yourself wondering about key #1? Did you notice that Tom didn't take time to create a compelling vision until his cholesterol results demanded his attention? His story is a great example because it brings up a point we haven't talked about yet.

What happens if you don't take time to create a compelling vision? Life. Life happens anyway, but it may not be the life you want. Suppose you go through the next few years without creating a vision for your life after 50. Eventually, you'll wake up and find yourself—where? Living a life that makes you feel happy and fulfilled? Or reacting to problems that might not have come up, if only you'd created a vision and taken the steps to make it come true?

Sometimes life comes along and gives you a little nudge in the right direction. That's what happened to JoAnn, an active 68-year-old volunteer, mother, and grandmother from Louisville, Kentucky. JoAnn was having some long-term dental work, and the ongoing procedures left her mouth sore and uncomfortable. She found it difficult to eat because of the pain. After a short time, she noticed she was losing some weight. "This really isn't that hard," she observed. "I really haven't been doing without that much food, but the weight's coming off." It was just the incentive JoAnn needed. It showed her that she could lose weight and it wouldn't be that difficult. With an easy win under her now-looser belt, she was motivated to learn more about good nutrition, develop healthy eating habits, and continue losing weight until she reached her desired goal.

When it comes to your physical health, you could skip the compelling vision and eat what you want, exercise when you feel like it, and live only for the moment. But don't be surprised when those extra pounds start piling up, your joints get stiff from lack of activity, and your energy level plummets through the basement. If you don't create a compelling vision about your physical body and act upon it today, you'll find yourself having to *react* later, like Tom did with his cholesterol. Don't wait for circumstances to thrust themselves upon you. Don't wait for life to deliver your wake-up call. Take time to vision about your physical condition. And you know what they say: There's no time like the present.

I hope the visioning exercise in the last chapter helped you create a compelling vision for your physical body. Since you need both exercise and good nutritional habits to attain good physical health, you can use that same vision here as well. As a brief review, consider the following questions and keep your vision firmly in mind as you read the rest of this chapter.

- *Let your mind go wild!* How do you see yourself at 60, 75, or 100 years old? What do you look like? What can you do? How long do you think you might live if you achieved your ultimate physical condition?

- *Involve all five senses.* If you envision yourself at your peak physical condition because you've adopted healthy nutrition as your way of life, *see* yourself looking the way you'd look. *Feel* what it would be like to stand, sit, and move in a healthier body. *Hear* the comments your friends and family would make when they see you displaying your radiant health. *Smell* and *taste* each nutritious bite of the delicious foods you'd be eating.

- *Practice, practice, practice.* Remember, strong mental pictures lead to better results. Once you've identified a compelling vision for your physical condition, come back to it often. See yourself making healthy choices at the supermarket, restaurant, and dinner table. See yourself standing in front of the mirror or walking down the street in the body you desire. Don't forget, when you practice the results enough times in your head, taking the steps to achieve them becomes easy and automatic.

When Tom realized his cholesterol was high, he created a compelling vision. Sure, it would have been better if he'd done it sooner and avoided high cholesterol in the first place. In fact, I hope you'll learn from his example and commit yourself to a lifetime of healthy nutrition before you find yourself reacting to problems. However, as the old saying goes, it's better late than never. No matter where you are in terms of your nutritional status, it's never too late to turn things around, and the first step is creating a compelling vision.

Key #2: Connect Your Vision to Your Values, Passion, and Purpose

During the course of his interview, Tom relayed an interesting story about one of his coworkers. "This guy was about a hundred pounds overweight," he explained. "Similar kind of story to mine. He went to the doctor for a checkup and the doctor said, 'If you want to see your new grandchild graduate from high school, you've got to change a lot.' Suddenly, this ex-jock had an achievable goal. He said, 'I want to be around for the grandkids,' so he converted an extra room into an exercise room and totally changed his eating habits. In less than a year, I bet he's lost over 50 pounds and he's really looking good."

The doctor in Tom's story was a very wise man. He recognized one of his patient's most cherished values and helped him connect it to his nutritional needs. The patient wanted to be around for his new little grandchild. In fact, he wanted much more than that: He wanted to impact the child's life and dance at the little one's wedding someday. By tying his values to his vision—by picturing himself on that wedding day—he suddenly found the motivation to eat well, exercise regularly, and shed those extra pounds.

What are your most cherished values, passions, and purpose in life? Reflect on them for a few minutes and think about how you can connect them to your vision and your eating habits. Here are a few examples to help get you started.

- ***If you value contribution,*** improving your eating habits can lead to better health, more energy, and the ability to contribute even more in life.

- ***If you value knowledge and learning,*** you might enjoy learning about nutrition and the foods you eat.

- ***If you value accomplishment and achievement,*** think about how great you'll feel when you achieve the best physical health you possibly can and accomplish the goals you set for yourself.

Before we leave the subject of values, I'd like to recommend adding one more to your arsenal, if it's not already there. To make healthy eating a way of life, you'll need an attitude of patience and a long-term approach. When it comes to good nutrition, patience is one of the most helpful values you can possibly have. Interestingly, it's the exact opposite of the mentality that embraces the latest quick-fix, fad diet available.

You may have noticed that none of the preceding discussion included consulting the latest fad diet book to lose weight quickly. The reason is simple: No matter who wrote the book, or what it recommends, short-term diets are doomed to failure. Here's why:

1. *If a diet claim sounds too good to be true ("This pill magically melts away fat!"), it probably is.* Most fad diet books combine a bit of truth with a lot of speculation, even fallacy. If you could lose weight by taking a pill or by eating or not eating certain foods, everyone would be slender and no one would need the next fad diet book.

2. *A diet that works for one person (the famous author) may not work for everyone (you).*

3. *Fad diets may cause damaging side effects that the author may not yet know about.* For example, a fad diet could put extra stress on your kidneys or liver. As you get older, your body tolerates less abuse. A teenager may be able to "recover" from a fad diet much faster than a 50- or 60-year-old person.

4. *Fad diets steer you away from long-term, healthy eating habits and toward bad habits.* Some diets train your body to eat large amounts of one food or eliminate all types of another food, rather than eating moderate amounts of a variety of foods. This rarely works. Even when it's your favorite food, you'll eventually get tired of it and lose interest in the diet. Conversely, if the diet forces you to give up

a food you like, you may spend all your time craving that food and compensate for its loss by overeating other foods.

The bottom line: Achieving your nutritional goals requires patience and commitment to a lifestyle of healthy eating. Don't be one of those people who embraces the sentiment I once saw on a refrigerator magnet: "God grant me patience, and I want it now!" Forget the fad diets and add patience to your values, and you'll increase your chances of long-term success.

Key #3: Educate Yourself and Find a Great Coach

When it comes to health and nutrition, most Americans are woefully undereducated. Is it any wonder? Keeping track of all the vitamins, minerals, additives, and ingredients found in foods and beverages is no easy task. How do you know what's healthy and what's not? What's the secret to maintaining a healthy weight and body size?

For me, it's being lucky enough to have married a woman who's not only health conscious herself, but who also happens to be a registered dietitian. I'm only half joking when I say that the secret to my good eating habits is asking my wife, Kim, to plan our meals and order for me in restaurants. Now, you could marry a dietitian, or you could become an expert yourself, but either approach could take quite a while. Instead, why not follow key #3: educate yourself about the basics and find a qualified coach if you need additional help. Your education can start right now, because I'm going to share my good fortune and teach you everything I've learned from Kim about eating and enjoying a healthy, nutritious diet.

A Guide to the Basic Nutrients

I'm sure you'll agree that it's practically impossible to have good health without getting all the nutrients your body needs to function properly. In addition to keeping you healthy, good nutrition helps you look and feel better every day. When you know how to make good nutritional choices, you can enjoy eating.

To keep your body healthy, you need to ingest certain nutrients every day:

- *Macronutrients* (proteins, fats, and carbohydrates) provide calories and supply the body's basic building blocks. Fluids are also included in this group, because they serve essential functions as well.

- *Micronutrients* (vitamins, minerals) don't provide calories but they help regulate body processes.

- *Phytochemicals* don't provide calories and aren't classified as traditional nutrients, but they're biologically active compounds that may play an important role in health.

Macronutrients

Proteins provide amino acids, the building blocks your body uses to create and repair such things as enzymes, muscles, and red blood cells. According to the new Dietary Reference Intakes (DRIs), the protein you need (about 10 to 35 percent of your total calories) should come from protein-rich foods like fish, poultry, lean meat, beans, tofu, eggs, and nuts, plus dairy products like nonfat or low-fat milk, yogurt, and cheese.

Carbohydrates are your body's primary energy source, providing the calories you need for immediate use. You can get most of the carbohydrates you need (about 45 to 65 percent of your total calories) by eating fruits, vegetables, and whole-grain products (including bread, cereal, pasta, and rice). Carbohydrates can be simple, like table sugar, or complex, like the carbohydrates in whole-grain products, vegetables, fruits, and beans. Complex carbohydrates are your best nutritional choice, since, in addition to supplying energy, vitamins, and minerals, they can supply fiber. For optimal health, you need 25 to 35 grams of fiber each day.

Fats serve three different functions. They store energy, insulate body tissues, and transport fat-soluble vitamins through the blood. However, researchers have linked increased fat intake to heart disease and cancers, and they've discovered that the type of fat you eat is just as important as the amount.

To get the fat you need, choose mostly foods that contain *unsaturated fats*—the "good" fats that may help lower LDL ("bad") cholesterol and decrease your risk of heart disease. These include:

- ***Monounsaturated fatty acids,*** which are found mainly in vegetable oils such as canola, olive, and peanut oils. They are liquid at room temperature.

- ***Polyunsaturated fatty acids,*** which include omega-3 fatty acids and are found mainly in vegetable oils such as safflower, sunflower, corn, flaxseed, and canola oils, and in seafood. They are liquid or soft at room temperature.

Limit your intake of the "bad" fats, which may increase your LDL and total cholesterol levels, putting you at risk for heart disease. These include:

- ***Saturated fatty acids,*** which are found in animal sources such as meat and poultry, whole or reduced-fat milk, and butter. Some vegetable oils like coconut, palm kernel oil, and palm oil are also saturated. Saturated fats are usually solid at room temperature.

- ***Trans fatty acids,*** which are formed when vegetable oils are processed into margarine or shortening. Dietary sources include some dairy products, as well as snack foods and baked goods made with partially hydrogenated vegetable oil or vegetable shortening. Trans fatty acids may also lower HDL ("good") blood cholesterol levels.

Some people make the mistake of increasing their "good" fats more than they should, resulting in unwanted and unexpected weight gain. Remember, even the "good" fats contain calories.

No more than 20 to 35 percent of your total calories should come from fat, and no more than 10 percent of your total calories should come from foods high in saturated and trans fatty acids combined. Although 35 percent may sound high, people in Mediterranean countries commonly ingest this amount, and studies suggest their diet is quite healthy and they have no increased risk of heart disease. However, most of the fat they eat comes from fish and olive oil rather than saturated or trans fat sources.

Fluids, especially water, provide three essential services. They hydrate the body, transport nutrients, and carry off waste products. Fluids are just as important to your health as the other macronutrients. In fact, you'd die much more quickly from dehydration than you would from malnutrition. The best way to get the fluids you need is by drinking eight to ten 8-ounce glasses of water a day (more if your weight or activity level increases or you're outside on a hot day) and occasionally drinking other caffeine-free, nonalcoholic beverages. Be careful, though. Although all beverages provide fluids, those with caffeine and alcohol can actually make your body lose some of its water. If you include these beverages in your diet, make sure you have a good balance and an adequate overall intake of fluids.

Micronutrients

Vitamins help enzymes perform and regulate your bodily processes. Each vitamin plays a specific role in your body; one cannot substitute for another. Some vitamins are water soluble and must be replenished daily. Others are fat soluble; since they stay in the body longer, you need less of these.

Like vitamins, *minerals* (such as calcium, phosphorus, magnesium, iron, zinc, and copper) help regulate bodily processes, and they help the body hold together its cells and tissues. Vitamins and minerals may have yet another function: Researchers are currently exploring their role in disease prevention. For example, there have been literally hundreds of studies on the antioxidant properties of vitamin A (beta carotene), vitamin C, vitamin E, and selenium. While the data is still inconclusive, most of the research that shows a protective health effect shows that eating foods rich in antioxidants is more effective than taking supplemental forms.

Phytochemicals

Phytochemicals are plant substances (for example, isoflavones in soybeans and lycopene in tomatoes) that help your body build immunity against illnesses like heart disease and cancer. More than 900 phytochemicals have been identified so far, and research continues into this relatively new area. Unlike vitamins and minerals, phytochemicals have not been proven essential for keeping you alive. In fact, there are no recommended daily allowances (RDAs) for phytochemicals. However, emerging scientific evidence suggests they may play an important role in determining your quality of life.

To summarize all this complex information, let me remind you of something you've probably heard since you were a small child. It's just as true now as it was back then: The best way to get all the nutrients you need, in their most effective forms, is to eat a wide variety of foods each day. Remember, almost every food contains some of the nutrients you need, but no one food contains them all.

When to Consult a Professional

Even though I started this section by suggesting you marry or become a dietitian, I hope you know I was only kidding. Obviously, you won't need professional nutritional advice every day, but there may be times when you need guidance you can trust.

Tom, the man with high cholesterol, consulted Kim about changing his diet. Armed with additional knowledge, he quickly realized he'd been getting empty calories and too many fats from the foods and beverages he routinely chose. "You get into a habit," he observed. "Come home from work, open up a bottle, have a glass of wine. There's a lot of calories, as I found out." Or he'd go to the country club on "steak night" and automatically order a steak. "But there's also three kinds of fish," he discovered. "Ever since I started this, I've always had fish. I'm trying different kinds of fish I've never even had. Like grouper. I'd never had it and now I love it." With Kim's professional guidance, Tom uncovered his hidden problem areas and devised effective solutions.

After losing her first few pounds due to dental pain, JoAnn tried one of the no-carb diets so popular today. She read the book and followed the diet religiously for the first two weeks, then decided to modify it. While I don't advocate this type of diet at all, it did serve one useful purpose: JoAnn learned some nutritional basics and realized she'd been eating excessive amounts of starchy foods.

Diet books such as the one JoAnn chose typically contain one or two morsels of useful information. However, if you want to get your guidance from a book, please choose one that's based on sound nutritional principles. Ask your doctor or dietitian for their recommendations, or consult the American Dietetic Association's (ADA) Web site at www.eatright.org. This valuable site includes a recommended reading list, links to government resources, and excellent nutrition fact sheets, including one called "Popular Diets Reviewed." The site even offers a search feature that lets you type in the name of a particular diet or other key words and get a list of related articles and information. You'll also find several excellent sources for nutritional information in the Recommended Reading list at the end of this book, as well as periodic updates on the www.nevertooold.com Web site.

Although the Internet can be an important source of information these days, please be aware that some Web sites are more reliable than others. Stick to the sites maintained or recommended by reliable, professional organizations such as the ADA. You can also find additional information through the consumer information programs at major nutrition-oriented universities.

Sometimes, it takes more than nutritional information, coaching, lifestyle changes, or willpower to regain control of your eating habits and achieve your desired goals. If you're having difficulty keeping up your exercise schedule or taking off excess weight, an undiagnosed medical condition could be the cause. Thyroid problems, diabetes, heart disease, and clinical depression are among the many disorders that can affect the way you feel, eat, or metabolize food. Undiagnosed medical, psychological, and emotional conditions require professional attention. Mickey, a 51-year-old surgical nurse, found that out the hard way.

Ten years ago, Mickey was juggling four children, working with her husband in his surgical practice, and going through perimenopause when her daughter developed an immune deficiency that kept her from attending school. Mickey decreased her work hours to home-school her daughter and give her the care she required. Four years later, the same daughter received a severe head injury that caused physical and emotional damage. "It's been an all-consuming process for me," Mickey explained. "When that happened, I stress ate. I used to walk every day; I stopped walking and just really took care of my child. I'm sure I got incredibly depressed. I ended up putting on an additional 50 pounds."

One day, Mickey experienced a life-changing realization. "When you're in an airplane, one of the things they tell you is to put on your oxygen mask first and then assist your child or neighbor. It just smacked me right in the head. I realized that if I didn't start taking care of myself, I wasn't going to be around to take care of anyone else."

Mickey was wise enough to seek professional help. "About three years ago, the doctor ended up putting me on an antidepressant to help me with just being able to get my left foot in front of my right. I think it probably also had some appetite suppressant quality to it. As my desire for food went down and my activity level increased, the weight just started coming off."

Unlike some people who think, *Okay, I have this problem so it means I'm going to be heavy,* Mickey got the help she needed, and then she took additional action. Over the next two and a half years, she changed her eating habits and lost all the weight she'd gained, plus some.

"I think you have to do this for yourself," she said. "You can't do it because of all the extreme makeovers on television, the way the magazines are, or the way people are portrayed to be perfect, whatever perfection is. It's a case of self-love. You have to love yourself, like yourself, and be kind to yourself. I think that two things we have a very difficult time in this world accepting or understanding are that it's okay to have help, and basically you have to love yourself.

"This was a decision for my life," Mickey added. "When you're totally engaged with your kids and everything, you can't really think about life beyond. But that can be absolutely the most wonderful time of your life. I want to soak that up and love every bit of it. There are things I want to do—horseback riding, gardening. When you're overweight, you don't realize how difficult it is to be able to breathe, to be able to walk."

Please follow Tom, JoAnn, and Mickey's examples and seek qualified professional guidance if any medical, emotional, or nutritional issues may be affecting your quality of life.

Finding a Qualified Nutritional Coach

When you need nutritional advice you can count on, start by asking your family doctor or healthcare provider. However, don't be surprised if they refer you to a registered dietitian.

A registered dietitian, or RD, is your best source of reliable nutritional information. Just as your doctor specializes in the diagnosis and treatment of disease, an RD specializes in nutrition.

Please don't confuse a nutritionist with a registered dietitian. A registered dietitian is a trained professional in a highly regulated field. It takes a minimum of a bachelor's degree from an accredited college or university, followed by an intensive, supervised internship and a rigorous qualifying examination, to become an RD. Many even have master's degrees in nutrition. While some RDs may call themselves nutritionists, a nutritionist is not necessarily a registered professional. A nutritionist may not have any of the credentials of an RD. People can call themselves nutritionists after taking only one course in nutrition. They may even work at health-food stores, which is a clear conflict of interest.

A Typical Consultation

An RD can help you separate facts from fads and interpret the wealth of nutrition information available. You can, of course, call a registered dietitian to ask a single nutrition-related question. However, if you want the RD to design a custom nutrition plan tailored to your needs and personality, you'll need to establish a longer relationship.

A typical consulting relationship might involve your meeting with the RD once a week for the first two or three sessions, then once a month for up to a year. The weekly sessions can establish your basic nutritional program; the monthly sessions serve as a follow-up to gauge the program's effectiveness and perhaps update it as needed.

For a referral to an RD in your area, contact the American Dietetic Association at 800.366.1655, or visit www.eatright.org and enter your Zip code in the "Find a Nutrition Professional" field on the home page.

Making Sense of Nutritional Information

There's one more information source you'll probably run into. In today's fast-paced information age, each new research discovery is likely to become the leading sound byte on the six o'clock news. I'm sure you've heard headlines like, "Latest research will radically change the way we eat." One day, you're told to eat more protein;

the next day, less. Then it's, "Eat all carbohydrates and no fats," or "Eat the 'good' fats and avoid the 'bad' fats," each with long, unpronounceable names. No wonder it all seems so confusing.

If you listened to everything you heard, you'd either be eating large quantities of everything or eating nothing at all. Since neither of these is really an option, here are some suggestions for evaluating the next nutrition-related story you read in the newspaper or hear on TV.

- *Look at each newly reported finding as an interesting tidbit,* not necessarily a reason to change the way you eat. Nutritional guidelines do change over time, but no one study is enough to change well-established guidelines.

- *Remember that nutrition is a relatively young and slowly evolving science.* The most reliable nutritional studies take several years to conduct, include information from a large number (even thousands) of people, and are conducted by respected universities.

- *Don't get advice from someone who has something to sell you.* Even a good health-food store can't provide unbiased advice. The nutritionists at the store may seem knowledgeable, but they'll be inclined to promote foods and supplements from that store. The diet guru on the cover of the latest book may look trustworthy but may give advice that only sells more books.

- *If you hear about a study that interests or concerns you, find out how medical professionals react to the study.* Call your doctor, healthcare provider, or registered dietitian to get his or her opinion.

Educating Those Around You

When it comes to changing your eating habits, you may not be the only one who needs some education. JoAnn discovered this when she tried to lose weight: "People hound you to get you to eat," she said. "Did you ever notice that?"

We Americans are such social eaters. We invite each other into our homes and offer food as if it were a gift. Then we're insulted if anyone turns us down.

Teaching people not to be offended if you don't eat their food may require some patience and discipline, but it's well worth the effort. Tell them you're training for healthy longevity, and maybe they'll decide to join in.

Key #4: Formulate and Implement a Healthy Eating Plan

"One should eat to live, not live to eat."
—Jean-Baptiste Moliere, 17th-century actor and dramatist

When it comes to formulating a plan, remember these three words: measurable, attainable, and *simple.* I'm not one to weigh, measure, calculate, and agonize over what I can and cannot eat, and I don't advocate that kind of diet. No food is inherently good or bad; you should simply eat more of some foods and less of others. The best way to eat involves a long-range approach that includes a variety of healthy foods every day.

However, there is one exception. When you're getting started, you may need to count calories or fat grams, keep a food journal, or find some other way to get an accurate picture of the amount and types of foods you eat.

Ed, the 71-year-old retired marketing vice president you met in chapter 3, described his experience with calorie counting. "There was a period of time back in my 40s or early 50s," he said, "when I was eating a big bowl of ice cream every night. I finally figured out that's more grams of fat than you're supposed to have in a whole day. So I started eating smaller portions and switching to low-fat ice cream or yogurt. More recently, I've discovered that counting grams of fat doesn't work anymore because of what the food manufacturers have done—and I've looked at myself as having been in the food business all my life. To replace fat, guess what's the number one substitute? Sugar. So now I'm counting calories instead of grams of fat."

As I said, I don't advocate weighing and measuring foods, but I urge you to do it at first if it helps provide a realistic picture of exactly what you're eating.

The next step is to create a plan with measurable results. What do you hope to accomplish and in what period of time? What are you willing to do to accomplish your vision and goals? The more specific and measurable you make your plan, the better chance you have of staying on track and ensuring your success. A measurable plan might include specific targets such as eating five servings of fruit and vegetables each day; drinking eight glasses of water; or reaching specific targets you set for your cholesterol, triglyceride, or blood pressure levels. Your plan should include clearly stated goals, such as not going above a certain dress or belt size, or being able to walk or run a certain distance in a specific amount of time.

One final thought on the subject of measuring. Focusing all your attention on how much you weigh can sometimes be a deterrent. Kim notes, "I've worked with a lot of people who weigh themselves every day, sometimes twice. One of the first things I tell them is, Don't! It's unhealthy. Their goals are often unachievable, due to a number of different factors. If tracking your weight is a negative for you, forget about the scale and find something else to shoot for."

Tom, our cholesterol-conscious example, took Kim's advice and achieved excellent results: "I don't weigh myself. I did this to work on other markers and to see what would happen on the other side. All I can tell you is I've lost a lot of weight."

Don't wait until you're sick or overweight to formulate a healthy eating plan. Start now to build your long-term health by following these simple nutritional guidelines.

A Six-Step Eating Plan

1. ***Watch your portion size.*** The key elements of a nutritious diet are moderation and balance, not elimination. You can eat almost anything as long as you eat moderate amounts. For example, U.S. Department of Agriculture (USDA) guidelines allow you to eat up to two servings from the meat group a day. However, a serving means 2 to 3 ounces of cooked steak, not the 24-ounce sirloin some restaurants offer.

2. ***Eat at least three times a day.*** Don't skip meals, even if you have to eat on the run or at your desk. The body works best when it receives fuel throughout the day; it doesn't run well on empty. When you finally eat after skipping a meal, your body may crave sugar (for quick energy) and fat (as insurance against future missed meals).

3. ***Control your weight with a combination of healthy eating and adequate exercise.*** As always, before beginning any weight-loss program, or if you have questions about your appropriate weight and body fat, please consult your doctor or a registered dietitian.

   If you want to lose weight, don't focus on a particular number ("I need to weigh 130 or I'll die"). You may never reach your "ideal" weight if you base that ideal on unrealistic expectations. If you've never weighed 130 in your adult life, your genes may not allow you to weigh 130 and be healthy. Instead, decrease your portion size and increase your exercise until you reach a healthy body mass index, or BMI.

   According to the National Institutes of Health, BMI is a measure of body fat based on height and weight. It is a reliable indicator of total body fat, but it has two limitations: It may *overestimate* body fat in athletes and others who have a muscular build, and it may *underestimate* body fat in older persons and others who've lost muscle mass.

How to Calculate Your BMI

$$\frac{\text{weight (lb.)}}{\text{height (in.)}^2} \times 703 = \text{BMI}$$	Underweight ... Below 18.5
	Normal 18.5–24.9
	Overweight 25–29.9
	Obese .... 30+

Source: National Center for Chronic Disease Prevention and Health Promotion

For example, a five-foot, eleven-inch man who weighed 175 pounds would calculate his BMI this way:

$$\frac{175 \text{ lbs.}}{(71 \text{ in.})^2} \times 703 = 24.4$$

4. ***Don't punish yourself for an occasional overindulgence.*** Just think of it as one big meal (or one big piece of chocolate cake), not a mortal sin. Tomorrow's a new day.

5. ***Enjoy eating.*** This is the most important step of all. Look at your diet not as a set of don'ts, but as a set of dos. Do enjoy a wide variety of foods such as tasty fruits and grains. Do indulge yourself with a luxurious restaurant meal occasionally. Do eat with passion, chewing slowly and savoring every flavor.

6. ***Use information from the USDA*** to learn how to eat a variety of foods, including a healthy amount of foods derived from plants. Using the nutritional information on food labels, adjust your intake of nutrients, calories, fat, salt, and sugar to meet USDA guidelines. (The USDA's new Food Guidance System, due out in early 2005, will include revised guidelines to help Americans choose a healthier diet.) Pay particular attention to your need for at least five servings a day of fruits and vegetables; many Americans ignore this aspect of a healthy diet.

Key #5: Monitor Your Plan and Update as Needed

When Kim and I were first married, I wasn't a big vegetable fan, and I really didn't care for salads. Obviously, my eating plan needed some modification. "How about if I take vitamins or minerals and skip all that green stuff?" I hopefully suggested.

Kim sat me down and patiently explained that there's just no way to meet my nutritional needs by substituting a pill—or multiple pills—for a healthy diet. She also taught me that there's no such thing as a natural vitamin pill; the natural way to get vitamins is from the foods we eat. Period. Instead, she introduced me to some delicious vegetable dishes and even convinced me to try some salads that included fresh fruits, nuts, and seeds to satisfy my sweet tooth. I'm living proof that you're never too old to learn to love vegetables, and my healthier eating habits have paid immeasurable dividends in terms of my energy, attitude, and overall good health.

While I'm at it, I might as well confess that I was also hoping to find a painless, easy way to build stronger muscles. I'd heard that protein and amino acid supplements could do the trick, but once again, Kim explained that protein and amino acid supplements alone would not build muscles. In addition, scientists don't yet know the long-term consequences of overloading your body with excess amounts of protein and amino acids, but the research suggests there may be a threshold to how much protein your body can use. To build strong muscles, you're better off eating plenty of protein-rich foods and a sufficient amount of calories to keep your body from using the protein as an energy source, and you need to increase the amount of exercise you get.

The ADA and the American Pharmacists Association echo Kim's advice: "Dietary supplements are intended to supplement the diet and are never an effective substitute for healthful food choices" (*A Healthcare Professional's Guide to Evaluating Dietary Supplements: ADA/APhA Special Report*, 2000). However, there are some instances in which supplementation may be appropriate. Consult your doctor about supplementation:

- *If you require a prescribed medication.* Drugs can interact with vitamins and minerals. For example, some drugs deplete the body's supply of potassium or cause you to retain more of some vitamins. Taking a medicine may make it necessary for you to take a certain supplement or add a certain food to your diet. Tell your doctor or dietitian what drugs and nutritional supplements you're taking. Better yet, show them the bottles containing your supplements, since it's easy to get confused about what's in a particular preparation.

- *If you suspect or know you have a chronic health condition (such as osteoporosis, anemia, or malabsorption disorders).* These conditions may cause you to need large amounts of a particular vitamin or mineral. Alternatively, a chronic condition may make even the modest amount of supplement in a common multivitamin harmful. When you talk to your doctor about your condition, don't forget to ask whether you should alter your diet or nutritional supplements.

- *If you want to take very large doses of a particular nutrient.* Suppose you decide to eat large amounts of protein or take large doses of B vitamins. Too much protein may not be good for your body. An excess of B vitamins can prevent other vitamins from performing their proper function. Consult your doctor or registered dietitian before tinkering with the finely tuned machine that is your body.

- *If you've received nutritional advice from your neighbor.* People often say things like, "My friend told me I need more vitamin E. It did wonders for her." Don't take supplements just because someone else does. Remember, two people may not react the same way to a food or nutritional supplement, even if they seem to share the same condition (such as heart disease or high blood pressure). Even if the supplement isn't harmful, it may not be helpful, either; you could just be wasting your money. Before you do what your neighbor does, ask your doctor or a registered dietitian.

If you lead a busy life and sometimes don't eat right, you may want to take a nutritional supplement, just to be on the safe side. If that's the case, follow these guidelines to get the most from your supplements.

- *Focus on the big picture* (your need for a variety of micronutrients) rather than on just one particular micronutrient. To make up for any deficiencies in your diet, take one multivitamin-multimineral pill a day. Choose one that supplies no more than 100 percent of the RDAs of a broad spectrum of vitamins and minerals. In most cases, taking one multivitamin-multimineral will do you no harm and could be beneficial. However, as with anything involving your health, be sure to consult a physician or a registered dietitian before taking any dietary supplement.

- *Remember, more is not necessarily better.* Don't assume that if you need a little of a particular vitamin, you can get more benefit by taking more of that vitamin. Your body is a finely balanced machine. Too much of any vitamin, especially the fat-soluble ones (A, D, E, and K), can upset that balance. Unless your doctor says you need extra amounts of a vitamin, take just one multivitamin-multimineral pill a day and eat a healthy, balanced diet.

- *Think of any herb or vitamin supplement as a medicine, and never exceed the recommended dose.* If your doctor prescribed one antibiotic tablet a day for 14 days, would you expect to get the same benefit by taking all 14 tablets in one day? Of course not, and your vitamin-mineral supplement is no different.

- *Be aware that dietary supplements are regulated by the Food and Drug Administration (FDA), but manufacturers have a lot of freedom in the way they list dosages, amounts, and claims.* Unlike drugs and food additives, which must meet strict federal regulations, supplements are governed by the Dietary Supplements Health and Education Act (DSHEA). Unlike drugs, supplements do not need FDA approval prior to being sold to consumers. To increase your chances of getting a good product, try to use supplements manufactured by companies that also make pharmaceutical drugs; those companies probably have good manufacturing practices (GMPs) in place.

For additional information about choosing and using supplements, consult your doctor, healthcare provider, or dietitian.

Start with Easy Wins and Build on Your Success

When changing or adapting lifelong eating habits, don't try doing everything at once. Start by giving yourself a few easy wins, then build upon your success.

Tom, our cholesterol-lowering friend, started by eliminating sweets. "For me, that was an easy thing to give up," he explained. "It's not even a temptation. It's a mindless habit." After a short time of enjoying success with that change, he tackled a more difficult habit. "I stopped eating between meals," he recalled. "That was a tough one, so I said, 'If I have to snack, I'll either eat an apple or popcorn with no butter.' That really helped me get through because there are times when you're just still hungry. If you're going to break the rule, you might as well break it a little, not a lot." After a few short months, Tom's easy wins became part of his healthy new lifestyle.

Key #6: Enjoy Your Abundance

> *"My greatest delight is to take a good bite."*
> —Dylan Thomas, Welsh poet

Like many things in life, the abundance that comes from good nutrition can take two different forms: enjoying the process and enjoying the results. When JoAnn recovered from her dental work and discovered a new way to eat, she realized she felt better than she had in many years. "After I cut out the big, heavy meals," she said, "I can't eat like that anymore. If I do, I'll be really miserable. I'll just feel so full, and it's not a comfortable feeling for me anymore."

Without realizing it, JoAnn had stumbled across the Zen philosophy known as mindful eating. In his book, *Anger: Wisdom for Cooling the Flames* (Riverhead Books, 2001), the renowned Buddhist master Thich Nhat Hanh describes mindful eating as follows:

When I eat, I enjoy every morsel of my food. I am aware of the food, aware that I am eating. We can practice mindfulness of eating—we know what we are chewing. We chew our food very carefully and with a lot of joy. From time to time, we stop chewing and get in touch with the friends, family, or *sangha*—community of practitioners around us. We appreciate that it is wonderful to be sitting here chewing like this, not worrying about anything. When we eat mindfully, we are not eating or chewing our anger, our anxiety, or our projects. We are chewing our food, prepared lovingly by others. It is very pleasant.

We Americans rarely eat mindfully. From the time we're small children, we're taught to eat what we're told and clean our plates. At school, we learn to eat lunch when the bell rings—even it's only ten-thirty in the morning. As adults, we act as though enjoying our abundance means eating everything in sight: giant steaks, enormous baked potatoes, and sinfully rich desserts. Supersizing has become an American way of life.

The Zen philosophy of mindful eating offers a gentler, more healthful approach. It teaches you to pay attention to how food makes you feel. To stop eating before you get full and bloated. To embrace the abundance of different kinds of foods. Mindful eating invites you to experiment with new tastes, ingredients, and recipes, and to enjoy your abundance by enjoying the process of eating. Eating should be a pleasure in life, not a burden or a negative. Enjoy the process by eating like the Italians do—slowly and with passion, taking time to enjoy a variety of flavors.

As your body responds to a steady injection of a variety of nutritious foods, you can start to enjoy the results. You'll achieve a level of health, vitality, and energy you may never have experienced before. Enjoy the way you look and feel every day. Take pride in the compliments you get from your friends.

Sometimes your newfound abundance appears in unexpected ways. Tom not only lowered his cholesterol, he also discovered a pleasant surprise. "I haven't had heartburn in a year," he said. "Not once. I never connected heartburn with weight, but there seems to be a correlation there." JoAnn, who lost 35 pounds and three dress sizes, enjoyed the benefit of added reinforcement: "I guess we all have egos. When you see your friends and they say, 'Oh, you look great,' that's a boost."

Wherever you are in terms of your nutrition, take time to appreciate and enjoy the abundance you have. Remember, you tend to attract what you focus on in life, so focus on your abundance and you'll attract even more. As you continue to make further progress, be sure to notice and appreciate each new benefit that comes your way.

Key #7: Leave a Lasting Legacy

Some people believe, "My mom had cancer, my dad had heart disease. It doesn't matter how I eat, drink, or exercise; I'm going to get what they had." They may be right. Heredity is an important factor when it comes to health. But what if they're wrong? What if those people actually develop a chronic disease *because* of the lifestyle choices they make? What kind of legacy will they leave? What will their children grow up believing? "My mom had cancer, my dad had heart disease, it doesn't matter how I eat . . ."

Research shows that controlling your nutrition, exercise, lifestyle, and stress all have a positive impact on health. Maybe you do have the genes for heart disease, but a healthy lifestyle could mean the difference between developing it at 50 or holding off until you're 70. Maybe you do have the genes for cancer, but being in great shape can help your body recover faster if you have to undergo surgery, chemotherapy, or other treatment forms.

You can't control everything, but you can control the way you eat. What kind of legacy is your current eating plan creating? Is it the one you want to leave? If not, now's the time to control the things you can and create different possibilities for yourself and those you love. Your legacy, and theirs, depends on it.

In the next chapter, we'll look at one last aspect of good physical health—taking responsibility for your own health care. However, please don't leave this chapter without spending a few minutes on the coaching questions that follow.

◆　◆　◆

Coaching Questions

Are You Practicing Good Nutrition?

- The best diet consists of a healthy variety of foods, eaten in moderation at least three times a day, for the rest of your life.

  Is your diet the best it can be? What areas could you improve to make life after 50 your best years yet?

- Enjoy eating! Focus on what you can eat (almost anything in moderation, for most people), not what you have to give up.

  Are you following the guidelines for basic nutrition outlined in this chapter? If not, what do you need to eat MORE of to make your diet healthier?

- When you need nutritional advice you can count on, start by asking your family doctor or healthcare provider.

  Where are you getting your nutritional advice? Is the information accurate, or do you need to find a better source?

Chapter 6

BE THE CEO OF YOUR HEALTHCARE TEAM TO ATTAIN OPTIMAL HEALTH

In 1977, 49-year-old Mel Zuckerman was one of Tucson, Arizona's leading homebuilders. He enjoyed tremendous business success but suffered from a host of physical ailments, including overweight, asthma, high blood pressure, and hiatal hernia. He'd tried a weight-loss spa ten years earlier but hitchhiked out after just three days. Intellectually, he knew he should lose weight and manage his stress. Emotionally, it didn't seem important enough to try—until his father was diagnosed with lung cancer.

In the introduction to *The Canyon Ranch Guide to Living Younger Longer* (Simon and Schuster Source, 2001), Mel wrote, "My father had finally made the emotional connection between his behavior and his health. We buried him six months later. During those months I sat and talked with him every day. . . . Every conversation ended with him sitting with his head in his hands, moaning, 'If only I'd quit. If only I hadn't started. If only I'd listened. If only . . .' I can see him now. That was my 'Aha' moment—in time."

Mel, who hadn't walked more than a block in years, checked himself into what he described as "an old-fashioned fat-farm-type spa—they starved you, worked you out for five hours a day, and then gave you a massage." Ten days later, he ran a mile and a half in just over 11.5 minutes. He'd never felt so good and decided to stay a few more weeks. At the end of the third week, he called his wife and begged, "Please come out here. I've found what I want to do with the rest of my life and you have to see."

By the time they left the spa, Mel had lost 29 pounds and was running three miles a day. Less than two years later, he and his wife had liquidated their real estate holdings and used the proceeds to open Canyon Ranch Health Resort in Tucson, Arizona. They worked hard to make it a success, overcoming numerous obstacles along the way.

Today, with spas in four different states and onboard the *Queen Mary 2* luxury ocean liner, Canyon Ranch is widely acclaimed as America's premier health resort. In 2004, celebrating the resort's 25th anniversary, the healthy, youthful, 76-year-old Zuckerman has no plans to retire. He remains committed to his value of a healthy lifestyle and to his vision of sharing it with as many people as possible. If someone asks him what's most satisfying to him, Mel quickly replies, "My most gratifying moments are when guests tell me, 'I got it! Canyon Ranch helped me turn my life around.'"

Long before he became CEO of Canyon Ranch, Mel Zuckerman held a far more important position: CEO of his own health care. Just as Canyon Ranch needs a CEO to take responsibility for the activities of the business and its employees, each of us must accept the ultimate responsibility for our health. We can simplify this complex task by applying the seven keys and taking a proactive approach.

Health care today is a multifaceted and rapidly evolving field. To further complicate matters, American society has become increasingly mobile, with people frequently changing jobs and moving to new communities. Gone are the days of having the same family physician throughout your life. When you change jobs, you generally change healthcare plans. When you relocate, you have to find a new doctor. Today, it's more important than ever to be knowledgeable about your health and take responsibility for your care.

Key #1: Take Time to Create a Compelling Vision

*"Health is a state of complete physical, mental,
and social well-being, and not merely the absence
of disease or infirmity."*
—Constitution, the World Health Organization

Like Mel Zuckerman, you probably know that taking care of your health makes you feel better and benefits the people you care about most. If you aren't taking care of your health, it may be because you lack a compelling vision for your future years.

One of the first steps to making life after 50 your best years yet is recognizing the possibilities of an extended life span. I've said it before and I'll say it again: You're probably going to get old, whether you take care of yourself or not. Unlike all the king's horses and all the king's men, medical science now knows how to put you together again. Doctors and scientists have become experts at keeping people alive. Imagine what they'll be able to do 30 years from now, when you're 80 or 90 years old. If you have a hard time believing things will change much in the future, try looking *back* 30 years at how far medicine has come.

While medical science gets better at prolonging life, we Americans endanger our health by becoming overweight and failing to exercise. According to the National Center for Health Statistics, 61 percent of American adults are overweight and 27 percent are clinically obese. Unless we take better care of ourselves, we won't have the energy, fitness, and vitality to enjoy a great quality of life as we age.

Creating a compelling vision of your future life can propel you to take the actions needed to make that vision come true. Maybe you won't live to be 90 or 100, but what if you do? What kind of health would you like to enjoy from now until then? What quality of life do you want?

I often hear people say they don't want to get old, but they really mean they don't want to get sick, experience pain, or have to depend on others. If that's your vision of aging, it's time for a change. It's time to start believing that getting older means getting better, having more fun, and taking on new challenges—including challenges to your health.

Until recently, health was considered to be the absence of illness or disease, and most people didn't think about their health until they became ill. As you begin focusing on your vision for this area of your life, please consider a different definition. Think of health as the active pursuit of well-being, that sense of "feeling good" that seems to elude so many people.

In his book *Creating Health* (Houghton Mifflin, 1987), best-selling author and physician Deepak Chopra, MD, wrote, "Health is our natural state. The World Health Organization has defined it as something more than the absence of disease or infirmity—health is the state of perfect physical, mental, and social well-being. To this may be added spiritual well-being, a state in which a person feels at every moment of living a joy and zest for life, a sense of fulfillment, and an awareness of harmony with the universe around him." When approached from that perspective, health becomes a more comprehensive subject, encompassing all aspects of life.

Is such a vision of health possible? Yes, but it can't be left to chance. I challenge you to imagine a future where you'll feel as good at age 90 as a healthy, active 70-year-old feels today. I urge you to start taking care of your health in a way that creates the possibilities for you to enjoy those bonus years.

Turn Back the Hands of Time

As you create a compelling vision of your optimal health, here's an interesting idea to consider: Change your perceptions of time and age. Albert Einstein once said, "When you are courting a nice girl an hour seems like a second. When you sit on a red-hot cinder a second seems like an hour. That's relativity" (*News Chronicle,* March 14, 1949). In the same way, your perceptions of aging affect how you feel. If you think of age 65 as being old and decrepit, that's pretty much how you'll feel when you hit 65.

However, if you think of age 65 as being filled with new opportunities and a time to focus on yourself, you'll probably feel pretty good about reaching that age.

Here's a great tip to help change your perceptions about your age: Beginning today, think of yourself in terms of your biological age instead of your chronological age. If someone asked how old you were, you'd probably do what most people do—recite the chronological age printed on your driver's license. A more significant measurement is your biological age, which indicates how well your physiological systems are performing in your body. If you're not happy with your chronological age, there's not too much you can do about it. However, when it comes to your biological age, you *can* turn back the clock.

If you're 50 today and in good physical condition, you probably act like your parents did at age 35. That means your biological age may be much closer to 35 than to 50. Biological markers can be measured; your physician can recommend the appropriate tests. There's also a fun Web site at www.realage.com that offers some simple questionnaires you can complete online. At the end, it gives your "real age." If you find out you're younger than your driver's license says, congratulations and keep up the good work. If you learn that your biological age exceeds your chronological age, it's time to develop a more compelling vision and make some serious changes.

Choose Inspiring Role Models

Here's one final ingredient for successful visioning about your health. If your vision of a long healthy future is not supported by your peers, find a new peer group and new role models to emulate—people like Mel Zuckerman, Bob Hope, George Burns, Dick Clark, Jack LaLanne, and Mother Teresa, who remained active and inspiring far beyond age 50.

Look to your own family or community for people like Dwight and Anne, two of the most energetic octogenarians I've ever met. At age 84, Anne's volunteer work in the arts, politics, and numerous philanthropic organizations spans over 50 years; she currently contributes at least 25 hours a week. Dwight, age 87, is a semiretired forensic psychiatrist who still spends 10 to 15 hours a week consulting on court cases. What's their secret? Anne suggests, "Don't let anyone ever tell you that you're over the hill at any time."

Develop a compelling vision of optimal, vibrant health, and life after 50 can be your best years yet. Your vision need not be detailed or complex. Carol, age 66, summed hers up this way: "There are people who are 75 and ancient, and there are people who are 75 and young. I aspire to be on the young side of 75. I aspire to have a good life for as long as I live."

Mike, age 62, said, "When my first grandchild was born, I decided to dedicate the next 20 years to keeping myself physically fit so I could share my grandchild's college experience like I did with my daughters. I don't want to go in a wheelchair. I want to go to a fraternity or sorority party and rock and roll!"

Key #2: Connect Your Vision to Your Values, Passion, and Purpose

When you completed the values profile in chapter 3 and listed your most cherished values, was health one of them? If you overlooked it while doing the exercise, chances are you're overlooking your health on a daily basis. I strongly encourage everyone who reads this book to add health and fitness to your values list.

Do you consider growing older a value? Do you see any positives associated with aging, or do you, like most Americans, worship youth instead? If you answered yes to the latter question, I strongly encourage you to reconsider and add aging to your values list, as well.

Rabbi Zalman Schachter-Shalomi is a professor emeritus at Temple University and the founder of the Spiritual Eldering Institute. According to the organization's Web site, the Institute "is a multi-faith organization dedicated to the spiritual dimensions of aging and conscious living, to affirming the importance of the elder years, and to teaching individuals how to harvest their life's wisdom and transform it into a legacy for future generations." In an article titled, "Saging—Not Aging" (*In Context,* Winter 1994), Rabbi Zalman wrote, "If somebody says to me: 'I'm not happy about the way I'm growing old,' I talk to them about shifting from aging to saging. . . . Spiritual eldering carries with it special opportunities; it means acting as guide, mentor, and agent of healing and reconciliation on behalf of the planet, nation, tribe, clan, and family. We become wisdom keepers."

How would you feel each day if you focused on gaining sagelike wisdom, and then found ways to use it by serving others? I predict you'd be energized and would look forward to a future filled with health and well-being.

The Power of Faith

Are faith, spirituality, and religion among your most cherished values? If so, they can be vital tools when it comes to your health. Scientific research supports the idea that faith can transform health in deep and long-lasting ways.

Harold Koenig, MD, is the founder and director of Duke University's Center for the Study of Religion/Spirituality and Health. He is also an associate professor of psychiatry and behavioral sciences and associate professor of medicine at Duke University Medical Center. In his book, *The Healing Power of Faith* (Simon and Schuster, 2001), Koenig writes, "Over the years, our center's scientists have led over fifty major research projects on the relationship between faith and health. . . . Many of the Duke Center's studies have produced groundbreaking findings."

Koenig's findings about religious people can be summarized as follows:

- They have significantly lower diastolic blood pressure than the less religious

- They're hospitalized less often

- They're less likely to suffer depression from stressful life events, and if they do, are more likely to recover

- They have healthier lifestyles, tending to avoid alcohol and drug abuse, risky sexual behavior, and other unhealthy habits

- They have a stronger sense of well-being and life satisfaction, due in part to stable marriages and strong families

- If stricken with illness, they have significantly better health outcomes

- They have stronger immune systems

- They live longer because they're better protected from cardiovascular disease and cancer

For those who believe in the power of prayer, a process called *centering prayer* can help you develop or refine your vision of health and well-being. Reverend Sandra Michels, pastor of St. Francis-in-the-Fields Episcopal Church in Zionsville, Indiana, describes the process this way: "Centering prayer is part of all religious traditions. Praying means listening, and one way to get into a listening mode is through centering prayer. Repeat a phrase or word, and then focus on it. As you time the prayer with your heartbeat and your breathing, and concentrate on the prayer, your breathing will slow down and your senses will become more open and alert. The listening attitude makes it possible to hear."

Whether you use prayer, spirituality, or any of the other methods described in this book, opening yourself to a vision of new possibilities and making the commitment to become CEO of your health can pull you out of bed each morning, energized with the courage to live your highest purpose based on your most cherished values. Then, aligning yourself with your destined greatness, you can lay your head on the pillow with peace of mind each night as you retire.

Key #3: Educate Yourself and Find a Great Coach

The long-running TV program *American Bandstand* was a powerful symbol of the rock and roll revolution. Of all the famous people of this generation, the show's host, Dick Clark, stands out as a supreme example of someone who defies the aging process and seems to improve over the years. With the energy of a perennial teenager dancing to the top hits, Clark still exudes vitality as the host of our national New Year's Eve party. Every year on that night, my wife and I join 10 or 12 couples for dinner at the home of our good friends, Mike and Mary, then we all gather around the TV to watch Dick Clark and see the ball drop in Times Square. Still inspired by Dick's charisma and authentic message of hope, we're reminded that, with the right attitude, next year can be even better, and we're never too old to rock and roll.

Even more impressive than his youthful appearance is Dick's recent willingness to talk about his health. Appearing on the Indianapolis-based television program *Healthy Living with Teresa Tanoos,* Dick revealed that he has type 2 diabetes. "Ten or eleven years ago, I went to my doctor for a physical checkup and he said, 'Oh, you have a little high sugar going on here. You've got type 2 diabetes. We'll put you on a diet, you'll do a little more exercise, we'll probably get this thing under control,' and it didn't happen. He then put me on medication and we got it to a level where I can put up with it."

When Tanoos asked Dick how the disease impacts his life, he responded, "In all honesty, Teresa, it hasn't changed my lifestyle. But inside my head I realize that I've got to be definitely more serious about my diet. I've lost several pounds in the last couple of months, I've got another three or four more to go, and I do my exercise every day, which doesn't really please me, but I know I've got to do it."

When Tanoos asked why he's gone public about his disease, Clark replied, "Of late, they've come up with the statistic that two-thirds of the people with diabetes die of heart disease or stroke."

He continued, "Two-thirds of people with diabetes have no idea there's this correlation." As a result, Clark teamed up with the American Association of Diabetes Educators to inform the public about the heightened risk of heart attack and stroke for those with diabetes (check out www.knowtheheartpart.com). Armed with knowledge about their condition, they can take appropriate steps to decrease their risk and improve their overall health.

Remember, You're the CEO

Clark's experience shows the importance of becoming educated about your health care. Like him, you may face health challenges in the years to come. Life after 50 can be your best years yet, but that doesn't mean you won't get sick. No matter what you do about visioning, developing an exercise program, or keeping your diet on track, you may have to deal with illness or disease. Even if you make all the right choices, you could run into situations that rob you of your health or require treatment. If so, the most important thing you can do is become CEO of your healthcare team and work closely with your doctor and other providers to achieve the best results possible.

I cannot overemphasize the importance of educating yourself about any specific health concerns you may have. Nowhere is this more important than in the treatment of a specific illness or disease. If you suffer from an acute sickness or emergency, it might be okay to let the physician or nurse dictate, "Do as I say." However, with chronic diseases that require lifestyle changes, don't hesitate to discuss your questions and concerns with your healthcare providers. Remember, they work *for you!* You're the CEO. Get involved. Don't let the treatment plan develop without your input and participation.

Carlos Campos, MD, from the Institute for Public Health and Education Research, Inc., was speaking to the American Association of Diabetes Educators on August 14, 2004, in Indianapolis, Indiana. In diabetes care, he found that working as part of a team with the patient as an active participant is critical for improved health. He reported, "Involved patients show improved health behaviors, have fewer hospital stays, and have a shorter length of stay."

How can you become a more involved participant? Read, study, and surf the Internet for sources of information. Choose reputable sites such as the one run by the Centers for Disease Control and Prevention (www.cdc.gov). It features extensive information on health and safety topics. Your healthcare provider can also recommend sites for your specific area of concern. For detailed information on a particular topic, consult a university library. Their medical reference sections are usually outstanding.

Although you can't always rely on media information, do pay attention to reports of new developments in the medical field. Always consider the source and conduct additional research if you question the validity of any information you hear or read.

Find a Great Coach

When it comes to choosing a healthcare provider, you may feel somewhat restricted by your health insurance plan. People often say, "I'd love to try acupuncture or massage, but my healthcare plan won't cover it," or "I'd like to try a different doctor, but I have to use the ones in my HMO." I hope you remember our earlier discussion about opportunity risk. Please don't make the mistake of failing to use your money to enrich the quality of your health.

In your search for a qualified provider, don't hesitate to ask questions, read and study, and view your doctor as a valued coach. Simply put, a medical practitioner, therapist, or educator who acts as a coach is someone who will work with you as part of your team. Choose someone who believes in searching out the root cause of health problems and coaching you as you take the necessary steps to change your lifestyle and health choices. If you decide to seek nontraditional care, make sure there's scientific research to back up the approach you choose.

Dale, the 61-year-old adventurer you met in chapter 4, was playing squash one night and broke his leg. After a quick trip to the emergency room, he returned home in a wheelchair and cast. The next day, he arrived as usual at his oral surgery practice, where he was greeted by a new patient: an elderly woman accompanied by her daughter. As Dale ushered them toward his operating room, the daughter pulled him aside. "Don't worry about my mother," she whispered. "She's a little different. Just roll with the punches and accept what she does."

"Okay, I can do that," Dale replied, and the pair walked into the room. There they saw the mother, moving from one place to another and holding her wrist up to various items, apparently testing them in some way. She wore an odd-looking watch, something that looked like it could have come from a Cracker Jacks box.

"She tested the chair she was going to sit in, she tested the light, she tested the walls, and then she tested me," Dale recalled. "She finally said, 'That's good. You're okay. You'll be able to work on me because your polarity is correct.'"

Noticing his cast, the woman asked, "What's wrong with you?" Dale explained that he'd broken his leg the night before and it was somewhat sore and swollen. Then he performed the procedure she needed that day.

"The minute I had the tooth out," Dale recalled, "she reached into her purse and immediately pulled out a large sheet of heavy-looking material. One side was green and one side was red. She slapped the green side right over the area where I'd worked. 'What are you doing?' I asked. 'This magnet will take away all of my problems and make my mouth feel wonderful,' she said." Dale and the daughter glanced at each other, raising their eyebrows in disbelief. As the daughter had requested, Dale rolled with the punches and let the woman place the magnet on her face.

Later, as Dale was getting ready to leave for the day, a staff member stopped him. "The lady who used the magnet left a package for you," she said. Sure enough, the woman had left him a sack containing three magnets, which Dale described as small, medium, and gigantic. He put them in his briefcase and headed for home.

At about eight o'clock that night, Dale's leg was starting to throb. Nothing seemed to help so, on a whim, he asked his wife, Phyd, to bring him the magnets. He grabbed one and put the green side next to his foot. After about five minutes, the pain disappeared. "I'm not one for alternative medicine," he said, "so I left it on for ten or fifteen minutes and then I took it off." A few minutes later, his leg started to hurt again. He put the magnet back on and, once again, the pain disappeared.

"Oh, no!" he yelled.

"What's wrong? Does your leg hurt?" Phyd anxiously inquired.

"No," Dale answered grumpily, "it *doesn't* hurt! Bring me that big son of a gun!"

Did our oral surgeon friend become a believer in magnets? No, Dale didn't convert that easily. "There's no substitute for a double blind study," he insists. "For whatever it's worth, I still don't believe in magnets." However, Dale's story illustrates an important message for this chapter: Health care today is filled with new discoveries and alternative treatment forms. Read, study, and learn what's available. Be open to new ideas, educate yourself thoroughly, and obtain advice from a trusted coach.

Take a Proactive Approach to Your Health

The field of health care is so wide that I couldn't possibly present a basic overview as I've done in other chapters. However, I would like to briefly mention the concept of integrated medicine, which considers and treats patients from both traditional Chinese medical and traditional allopathic perspectives.

Dr. Young Ki Park is a board-certified family practice physician who specializes in both Chinese and osteopathic medicine. At his Westview Center for Integrated Medicine in Indianapolis,

Indiana, Dr. Park combines both treatment styles to offer his patients a natural approach to healing. "Most cases benefit from this combined approach," he says. "The medical perspectives of the two traditions represent two very different worldviews, but both can be used to heal the same body."

He offers the example of a patient he treated for extreme fatigue and obesity. From an allopathic perspective, her symptoms had no obvious cause. She had no problems with her heart, no strain in her neck, and no abdominal symptoms.

Dr. Park noted that her pulse was "lifeless" (thready, weak, hard to feel, almost nonexistent). She also had a very pale tongue. From the perspective of Chinese medicine, her weak pulse suggested a lack of *qi,* or energy flow within the body, and her pale tongue suggested a blood deficiency. Dr. Park treated her with a combination of herbs and other traditional Chinese remedies. However, he also suspected the patient had an underlying thyroid condition. After blood tests confirmed his diagnosis, he administered supplemental thyroid hormone in addition to the Chinese remedies he prescribed.

After treatment, the patient's energy level increased and she was able to exercise and lose weight. Dr. Park attributes her speedy recovery to his integrated treatment plan. "If I hadn't used Western diagnosis and treatment, I couldn't have helped her get her energy up as quickly," he says. "If I hadn't used Eastern diagnosis and treatment, I couldn't have addressed the underlying causes of her fatigue."

Dr. Park also recommends a proactive approach to health care. "You shouldn't wait until disease hits you. If you're proactive, you can actually reverse your biological age by actively pursuing a combination of balanced thinking, regular exercise, and healthy eating.

"No one else can take care of you," he tells his patients. "You must take care of yourself. Only you can adopt practices that promote and protect your total well-being. Only you can strive for balance in all aspects of your life."

Key #4: Formulate and Implement a Plan

As you consider your plan for making life after 50 your best years yet, ask yourself these three questions: Who am I? Where am I going? Who am I going with?

When you answer the questions in that order, you'll create a framework for making good decisions. Never, ever answer these questions backward. You run the risk of identifying with the roles you fill for others and losing perspective about who you are.

Frank, age 84, and his wife Betty Ann, age 82, are a testament to healthy living. You might remember them from chapter 4 as the couple who combined their love for traveling and their spirituality to produce an exercise plan aligned with their values. Frank and Betty Ann seem to be two people who truly improve with age. Frank, a psychiatrist, still sees patients about ten hours a week. He and Betty Ann play golf, use the computer, and ride their bikes to meetings and church events; they only stopped mowing their own lawn this year. Frank hopes to find a convenient clinic or group where he can volunteer his psychiatric services. Betty Ann, trained as a nurse, currently serves on a task force that's revolutionizing maternal-child care at Methodist Hospital in Indianapolis. I interviewed them not long ago and learned how they put the three questions to use in formulating a plan for a healthy life.

Who Am I?

Possessing a spirit of curiosity and vitality, Frank and Betty Ann have a definite understanding of purpose and meaning that allows them to define themselves from a deep level of the sheer enjoyment of being human.

Betty Ann said, "This business of living is an exciting thing. I hope I will grow old graciously when I start growing older. I'm going to fight when it's time to leave this place." Frank added, "We aren't going to leave here, we're going to be carried out."

This couple is wonderful to be around because they simply

love life and stay focused on the big perspective. They "don't sweat the small stuff" when difficulties come their way, which helps them maintain their healthy vitality.

Changes that create stress are a normal part of life. People who are distressed perceive change as something to be avoided. Those who embrace change are able to get over losses and challenges, heal, and move optimistically into the future. When I asked Frank and Betty Ann about their views on change, Betty Ann replied, "Thank God I'm here to see it." Frank added, "In a sense, we look forward to each one of the changes."

During our interview, I discovered that Frank had suffered a heart attack some time ago—one of those changes in health that can either break you down or improve your life. Betty Ann reflected on the event and gave this advice about learning from a health crisis: "There are two things not to ignore. One is the family history, and the other is ongoing good health. He had a coronary about five years ago, and all that coronary did was to make a little change. It was a glitch, a reminder, and it was wonderful. After it was over, it's just been marvelous. We've been much healthier since." This couple is adaptable, learns life lessons, and then keeps going.

Now, answer the question yourself: Who am I? By reaching as deep as you can go, discovering the answer to this question can bring stability and perspective as you ride the changes of life. Stay focused on the big picture, learn from each change and crisis, and your overall health will surely improve. Remember these words from the movie *The Natural:* "I believe we lead two lives. The life we learn with and the life we live with after that."

I once heard the story of a chaplain who was called to the bedside of an executive who'd just barely survived a heart attack. With tubes pumping medicines into his veins, and the beeping sound of the heart monitor in the background, the man turned to the chaplain and said, "I don't have time for this. I've got too much to do!" The chaplain paused for a moment, considering what words of wisdom he could share that would challenge this out-of-balance, type-A person to take better care of himself. Then he replied, "Do you remember the words of the psalmist: 'He *makes* me lie down in green pastures beside the still waters?' Could it be that your heart attack is a wake-up call that has forced you to lie down and be still?"

This story reminds me of the ancient Chinese character for crisis. With a few brush strokes, the word *crisis* is defined as both a challenge and an opportunity. Certainly for this man, and for each of us, the crisis of a heart attack could shake us up, challenge us to more fully appreciate life, and offer an opportunity for enlightenment about managing our health.

My message that life after 50 can be the best years yet invites you to embrace every event—even something as awful as a health crisis—as an opportunity to learn, grow, and discover more about who you are.

Where Am I Going?

Frank and Betty Ann know where they're going with life, even at age 84 and 82. When I asked them about retiring, they told me they were finally getting around to addressing the possibility.

Betty Ann said, "Retiring—that was where all this started from. I can remember my father's retiring, and I can remember, of course, Frank's parents retiring. They kind of retired *from* rather than *to,* and I think that makes a difference. Frank is retiring (so we say) so that we can do more traveling. We both like to travel, and we want to do it before we get too old and become a burden on other people when we travel. That's one of the reasons he's retiring. But another reason is that I'm his secretary, and all of a sudden, there's a lot of stuff that has to be done electronically. Though I've got a nice computer, I don't want to do it anymore. He's been talking about retiring for four or five years, so we finally came to the conclusion: My husband is retiring."

Most of the rock and roll generation won't retire as our parents and grandparents did. Instead, we have the choice to pursue new adventures, vocations, and avocations. The choices we make, based on our awareness of a life vision and purpose beyond our changing circumstances, can bring about a profound state of happiness and health.

What do you want to experience that would be an adventure? What would it take for you to achieve this goal? On a scale of 1 to 10, how likely are you to take the steps necessary to live out your dream? Are you committed to a vision of possibilities? What would be your first step in achieving your Big Hairy Audacious Goal?

As you contemplate the answers to these questions, consider the advice offered by the 13th-century Persian poet, Rumi: "Start a huge, foolish project like Noah. It makes absolutely no difference what people think of you."

Who Am I Going With?

Frank and Betty Ann have a strong sense of independent identity separate from each other. After 60 years of marriage, they also depend on one another to create a life of connectedness with each other, their family of six children and many grandchildren, and their friends.

"I don't think we'd live very long without the other one," Betty Ann said. "I think we're really mutually dependent. We do different things, we're very different people, but I'm not sure I'd want to live very long without him, and I'm sure he couldn't live very long without me. He's never learned to cook. We go out to dinner as much as possible, and when we're home, I cook and he cleans up. We've given up on trying to teach him to cook."

When asked about the secrets to their vitality and purpose, Betty Ann continued, "We're still very useful human beings. He's useful professionally; he's useful within the family. I too am useful. By useful, I mean needed. And I do an awful lot of things for a lot of people in the family. So feeling needed by the family and feeling useful is one of the keys."

Both Frank and Betty Ann offered one final piece of advice,

speaking practically in unison. "Keep healthy," Betty Ann said. "Keep physically active," Frank added. "Keep going and enjoy it," Betty Ann concluded. "Be useful. Not just feel useful, but be useful. That's a good place to be on this earth."

Key #5: Monitor Your Progress and Update the Plan as Needed

In the book *Dynamic Health* (Insight, 2003), Dr. Craig Overmyer suggests a daily practice for keeping your plan on track. In his work at St. Vincent's Hospital Center for Complementary Medicine and Pain Management, Craig discovered what he calls the 7 Response-abilities of Health-Wealth Investment. They're part of his Heal*thy* Living Coaching program. The word *Response-abilities* suggests that you have the ability to respond with a newfound creativity and insight to making decisions about your health.

Before you begin this exercise, find a quiet place for reflection, and have a pad and pen ready to capture your thoughts. Take about ten minutes from your daily routine to practice "conscious presence." Take a moment of pause, breathe deeply with awareness of your life breath filling your whole body, and then read each Response-ability, spending a minute or two anticipating some developing insight and wisdom.

The 7 Response-abilities of Health-Wealth Investment

1. Be Still; Wait Patiently for the Organizing Power of Wholeness

The very nature of life is a balance of rest and activity. By practicing stillness and learning to wait patiently, a renewed organizing power and energy will naturally result.

Are your health decisions fulfilling and in alignment with the highest possible outcome for your overall health and well-being?

2. Intentionally Declare Your Wants; Expect Needed Support

You have free will to make a multitude of decisions about what you want. Even if you don't get what you want, you may need to realize you're getting what you need.

Are you making health decisions today based on what you want or on what you need?

3. Surrender Old, Ineffective Patterns, but Never Give Up

Some habits and patterns give life, and some take away from life. Be willing to examine your patterns, surrendering any life-damaging thoughts, feelings, and actions, but never giving up on new disciplines.

Will you let go of destructive unhealthy patterns and begin new healthy ones?

4. Take a Courageous Stand; Affirm Your Most Cherished Values

By taking a stand for your health, you can face many challenges and tests. Be courageous to live your most cherished values. No one can take them away, and you'll be amazed at how energized you become by living your healthy faith.

Will you make health choices today that are in alignment with your most cherished values?

5. Just Do the Next Spontaneous Right Action, Guided by the Heart

With your values prioritized and your life purpose understood, set simple, measurable goals for your health today—just today. Make sure your heart guides you.

Are you simply focused on immediate goals that fit in with your long-term vision of health and well-being?

6. Honor Your Renewed Health Energy; Express Joy Always and Everywhere

Give thanks for all of life, including the troubles. Notice the joy of life, even if you're in the midst of a tough time. Be open to the lessons. Practice enduring joy for all things.

How will you celebrate the health you have today?

7. Energetically Serve Others; Be an Awesome Presence of Love

Get outside of your own health concerns and serve others,

without regard for the outcome. Research shows that by helping others, you immediately improve your own health.

Who needs your care and concern today?

Now that you've considered these 7 Response-abilities, take some time to write out any insights you've gained about your experience of health today. Make plans to implement actions that will improve your health or the health of others.

Key #6: Enjoy Your Abundance

"There ain't much fun in medicine,
but there's a heck of a lot of medicine in fun."
—Josh Billings, 19th-century humorist

This is serious—enjoying your abundance is good medicine and can improve your overall health. In a course called Living in the Endorphin Zone, business coach Steve Moeller asks participants, "How many of you have had a course on happiness?" Usually, no one raises their hand. Then he points out the vast array of scientific research about the human brain's ability to produce endorphins and enkephalins—secretions with morphine-like properties. These powerful substances course through your veins when you have the perception to enjoy life, practice happiness, and laugh much.

The field of medicine that addresses the influence of emotional states and nervous system activities on immune function is called *psychoneuroimmunology.* In essence, it states that your thoughts, feelings, beliefs, experiences, and attitudes create biological consequences.

This reality was dramatically described by Norman Cousins, editor of the *Saturday Review* for 30 years and an adjunct professor of psychiatry and behavioral science at UCLA. In 1979, he wrote *Anatomy of an Illness* (Bantam), which described his use of laughter to overcome a life-threatening form of arthritis. Cousins wrote,

"In August 1964, I flew home from a trip abroad with a slight fever. . . . Within a week, it became difficult to move my neck, arms, hands, fingers, and legs." His doctors eventually concluded that he was suffering from ankylosing spondylitis, which meant "the connective tissue in the spine was disintegrating." He was given a 1 in 500 chance of surviving.

"Up to that time," Cousins wrote, "I had been more or less disposed to let the doctors worry about my condition. But now I felt a compulsion to get into the act. It seemed clear to me that if I was to be that one in five hundred I had better be something more than a passive observer."

In other words, Cousins became the CEO of his healthcare team. After extensive research into his condition, he concluded that his illness was quite possibly caused by adrenal exhaustion, which could be caused by emotional tension, such as frustration or suppressed rage. Cousins wondered, "If negative emotions produce negative chemical changes in the body, wouldn't the positive emotions produce positive chemical changes? Is it possible that hope, faith, laughter, confidence, and the will to live have therapeutic value?" With those thoughts in mind, he formulated a plan for his own recovery, and approached his doctor with his ideas. "He shared my excitement about the possibilities of recovery and liked the idea of a partnership," Cousins wrote.

Since his condition involved severe inflammation of his spine and joints, pain relief became a primary goal. "I made the joyous discovery that ten minutes of genuine belly laughter had an anesthetic effect and would give me at least two hours of pain-free sleep." With the help of his physician, Cousins was able to quantify those results scientifically. His doctor "took sedimentation readings just before as well as several hours after the laughter episodes. Each time," Cousins noted, "there was a drop of at least five points. The drop by itself was not substantial, but it held and was cumulative. I was greatly elated by the discovery that there is a physiologic basis for the ancient theory that laughter is good medicine."

Cousins points out that laughter was not a substitute for traditional medical care, but he clearly demonstrated the role played by a full range of positive emotions—faith, hope, love, celebration, joy, purpose, meaning, commitment, vision, and courage.

Despite the odds against his survival, Cousins recovered from his illness and lived another 26 years before dying in 1990 at age 75. In one of his later books, *Head First: The Biology of Hope* (EP Dutton, 1989), he further described the power of the mind-body connection:

> If one asks, What are the primary influences on the immune system? the answer is, Practically everything. The immune system can be affected by biochemical changes in the body, by an invasion of microorganisms, by toxicity, by hormonal forces, by emotions, by behavior, by diet, or by a combination of all these factors in varying degrees. The immune system is a mirror to life, responding to its joy and anguish, its exuberance and boredom, its laughter and tears, its excitement and depression, its problems and prospects. Scarcely anything that enters the mind doesn't find its way into the workings of the body.

To make life after 50 your best years yet, you'll need a strong immune system. Focus your mind and heart on the very best life has to offer. Don't squander your abundance by forgetting the wonderful opportunity of life itself, each moment of every day. Remember the lessons demonstrated by Normal Cousins: As you enjoy your abundance, your health will improve.

Enjoy the Abundance of Nature

Many of us spend so much time inside buildings and cars that we forget to enjoy the wealth of nature and its abundant resources. Reconnecting with nature can bring renewed health and energy. Dr. Young Park, the practitioner of integrated medicine you met earlier in this chapter, reminds us to enjoy the abundant health benefits offered by three of nature's simplest wonders: sunlight, water, and air.

Sunlight

For several years now, experts have waged a huge debate about sunshine. How much is too much? Do the risks outweigh the benefits?

We know sunshine stimulates serotonin production and improves mood. It also assists in the manufacture of vitamin D, which helps the body absorb calcium, build stronger bones, and protect against illnesses like heart disease, rheumatoid arthritis, multiple sclerosis, and breast cancers. Furthermore, a recent study concluded that sunlight reduces the risk of developing a cancer of the lymphatic system that often affects people over 50.

In an article titled "Here Comes the Sun" (*AARP Bulletin*, June 2004), Nissa Simon reported, "When he began to study the relationship of sun exposure to non-Hodgkin's lymphoma, Bruce Armstrong, head of the University of Sydney School of Public Health, expected to find that the more time people spent in the sun, the more likely they were to develop the disease. To his surprise, men and women who got the most sunlight (other than those who worked all day in the sun) had the lowest risk."

Dr. Park calls sunlight a natural healer, and he recommends exposure to morning sun. "If you look at nature," he suggests, "you'll see that most animals, birds, and fish are most active early in the morning. Then they hide in the shade, because they intuitively know that afternoon sunlight is very damaging."

Your skin is your largest organ, and one of the most important for eliminating toxins and nitrogenous waste products. Damaging the skin through excessive sun exposure promotes premature aging. If you must be outdoors during peak sunlight hours, use sunscreen and wear a hat to avoid the sun's most damaging effects. If you live in a seasonal climate, take advantage of morning sunlight by exercising early, right after sunrise, for about 30 minutes to an hour. Exposure to morning sunlight can generate vitamin B, strengthen your skin, and help control your body temperature. Starting the day with some sunshine and exercise is a great way to experience and enjoy the abundance of nature.

Water

The human body consists of approximately 70 percent water. In Eastern medicine, water is considered the nurturing yin energy in the body. Dr. Park recommends that you drink water between rather than during meals, to avoid diluting gastric juices and allow the body to digest better. When the small intestine starts separating different nutrients, that's when you need water.

Don't just gulp water down; drink it slowly. Dr. Park offers this analogy: In the springtime, crops and trees gradually absorb water from a gentle, all-day drizzle. They thrive and experience their healthiest growth under those conditions. But when thunderstorms come, rivers flood, and everything washes away, the heavy rains often do more harm than good.

Similarly, drinking water slowly all day long helps to nourish your body. Take a sip of water in your mouth, let it become body temperature, then swallow. Remember to enjoy the abundance by drinking mindfully, appreciating each sensation and the gift of nourishment and good health you're receiving.

Air

Pain (neurological, musculoskeletal, or visceral) is due to a condition called *hypoxia,* which means decreased oxygen to the tissues and organs. Anytime you compromise the flow of oxygen to your cells, tissues, and organs, you experience pain.

To eliminate pain and prevent disease in the future, you must circulate oxygen and nutrients throughout your entire body. Practicing deep breathing and eliminating pollutions are important ways to do this.

Air is free, plentiful, and one of your most precious gifts. Enjoy the abundance and celebrate your good health with every breath you take.

Do Good for Others

This last concept may sound strange coming from a personal wealth manager, but doing good for others is probably as important as all the other healthful approaches described in this chapter. On the other hand, if you do harmful things, you may benefit initially, but in the long run, deep inside, it's going to eat you up and produce negative stress.

When you share your love, when you do good things, your body releases endorphins. You feel satisfied. And isn't that what healthy longevity is all about?

Key #7: Leave a Lasting Legacy

In this chapter, we've talked a great deal about appointing yourself CEO of your healthcare team and attaining optimal health. Obviously, doing so would be good for you. It would also be good for those you care about now and in the future.

You may be wondering how taking care of your health can be part of the legacy you leave. Mel Zuckerman has affected countless people who visit Canyon Ranch resorts. Frank and Betty Ann, the active octogenarians, set a wonderful example for their children, grandchildren, friends, and patients. Through his books and example, Norman Cousins has taught millions of people about the power of positive emotions.

You, too, will leave a lasting legacy, based on what you do with your life and how you take care of your health. Will you be a shining example for others to follow, or a glaring reminder of what to avoid? In general, there are two ways to learn:

- *The hard way:* By making your own mistakes or repeating the mistakes of others

- *The easy way:* By learning from positive role models and creating an empowering vision to achieve similar results

As you consider this concept of leaving a lasting legacy, which kind of example do you want to set? Will your children look at you and say, "Gosh, I don't want to die of lung cancer like my dad did. I'd better quit smoking." Or will they say, "Wow! Mom's still going strong at 90, living independently and having a great time. I want to follow her example and be just like her!"

If you haven't already done so, please take a few minutes to think about the kind of legacy you want to leave. Then appoint yourself CEO of your healthcare team and start making the positive choices that will allow your vision to come true.

By the way, if you really want to stretch your concept of attaining healthy longevity, visit www.livingto100.com and take the online survey. It was created by the Alliance for Aging Research, as a result of their Boston University Medical School-based New England Centenarian Study. The survey takes just a few minutes and provides excellent, science-based advice about what you can do to achieve your vision.

Now that we've talked about creating optimal physical health by focusing on your nutrition and exercise and becoming CEO of your healthcare team, it's time to look at creating the financial abundance to support a long and healthy life. Before you leave this chapter, though, please take a few minutes to review the coaching questions.

❖ ❖ ❖

Coaching Questions

Are You the CEO of Your Healthcare Team?

- Today, it's more important than ever to be knowledge-able about your health and take responsibility for obtaining adequate care.

  Who's in charge of your health? Are you the CEO, or have you delegated responsibility to someone else?

- Think of yourself in terms of your biological instead of your chronological age.

  How old are you really? Do you need to schedule an appointment to test your biological markers?

- As you consider your plan for making life after 50 your best years yet, you need a framework for making good decisions. Ask yourself these three questions:

  Who am I? Where am I going? Who am I going with?

Chapter 7

GET SERIOUS ABOUT YOUR MONEY: IT BUYS FINANCIAL FREEDOM

Entering the arena of personal finance and investing can be a stress-inducing experience. Why do most people view this area with such distrust? Having been in the personal finance and investment industry for 28 years and knowing the industry from the inside, I have some insight into that question.

Most of the professionals who enter the financial services industry are dedicated individuals who want to become trusted advisors and help their clients achieve their goals. However, in many cases, the industry suffers from inborn conflicts of interest and a win-lose business model that doesn't always put the client and advisor on the same side of the table.

The Truth about Financial Services

"Money is to be respected; one of the worst things you can do is handle another person's money without respect for how hard it was to earn."
— T. Boone Pickens, Jr., industrialist and philanthropist

When I became a stockbroker at age 24, I envisioned myself providing expert guidance to my clients about their financial concerns. In 1977, I'd just completed my Series 7 exam, the national licensing test that qualified me as a registered representative who could transact general securities trades. Eager to begin my career as an investment professional, I walked into my sales manager's office and said, "I just passed my exams. Now can you tell me what to do?"

He asked, "What do you mean, what do you do?"

"I mean, how do I do business?" I replied.

"You pick out a stock you like and get on the phone and start telling people to buy it!" he scowled.

That was the first part of my training. I went back to my desk and picked up a Standard and Poor's sheet on General Motors—the first company that came to mind. I thought of two or three reasons why the stock could go up, and then I started dialing numbers in the phone book. By the time I was ready to go to lunch, my shirt was soaked with sweat and I was wondering what I'd gotten myself into. This wasn't what I'd expected at all. I'd wanted to be a professional advisor, but stockbrokers aren't paid to give advice; they're commission-based employees who earn their money by moving securities and generating commissions. They earn promotions primarily because of their production, and less because of their competency. True, being a "big producer" often indicates some measure of competency, but not always. I quickly realized I was dealing with a dysfunctional business model and needed to find another way to provide professional service.

Financial Planning: A Step in the Right Direction

One day in 1979, my monthly copy of *Registered Representative* magazine arrived in the mail. The cover showed a man in a business suit, his open shirt revealing a Superman-type outfit with the letters *CFP* emblazoned across the chest. Inside, the article described a brand-new kind of advisor: a Certified Financial Planner. This highly trained professional helps clients tackle their most important issues—areas like estate planning, insurance needs, retirement goals, investment planning, and more. The idea instantly resonated with me, so I signed up for the program and spent the next year and a half earning my CFP designation.

Becoming a CFP was a step in the right direction. However, as a few years passed, I learned that while financial planning has many benefits, it doesn't always achieve its intended results. The model contains three inherent flaws:

1. ***Financial planners aren't usually investment experts,*** which means they rarely have professional designations in security analysis or portfolio management. Although there are some excellent planners who provide high-quality service, many focus on gathering financial data and producing a one-time, written plan containing future projections.

2. ***The fee structure tends to put more emphasis on the plan and less on the counseling.*** Planners generally charge a flat fee, a fee based on net worth, or an hourly fee. In most cases, planners put more emphasis on the planning process and less on financial coaching, client education, or counseling; this is partly due to the one-time, fee-for-plan business model. Some planners are fee- and commission-based, a model that causes them to focus more on implementing the part of the plan that requires buying products and less on non-commission-generating activities.

3. ***Financial planners typically refer the portfolio management duties to an investment management firm or mutual fund manager.*** The planner often charges a quarterly fee to "manage the investment managers," which means the client ends up paying layers of fees. In many cases, the planner does not have the expertise or specialized designations to justify the additional costs. With rare exceptions, the referred investment management firm or fund manager is not apprised of the client's personal objectives, tax concerns, or financial plan, resulting in a lack of coordination between the plan and the actual investment management.

One client, Mark, described an experience that illustrates some of the drawbacks inherent in financial planning. When Mark's wife decided to accept an early retirement offer, the couple had some decisions to make about the severance package she received. They consulted a financial planner who recommended that they invest in mutual funds.

Mark described the process this way: "Basically, it forced us to gather all our information in one location, and it forced us to look at our income, expenses, and tax liabilities, but that was something we could have done on our own. We never saw it as any kind of strategy. There was no real direction about what we should do to maximize income or minimize taxes. We had several accounts in several different places, but there was never any coordinated review of where things should follow. It was more of an organizational tool.

"With the financial planner," he continued, "we really didn't have any education. They picked certain mutual funds, but I had to ask for information about the stocks that the mutual funds invested in. They would have been perfectly comfortable just telling me what mutual funds they were going to invest in, and then I was supposed to sit back and watch what happened."

As Mark discovered, a typical financial planner attempts to predict whether you'll reach your investment objectives at a certain age, based on projected rates of return and inflation. "Of course, none of those things panned out," Mark observed, "because the rate of return didn't follow their projections, and there was really no follow-up, even though the projections immediately turned out to be incorrect."

Although Mark had selected a competent, experienced, and nationally acclaimed financial planner, the planner was constrained by a business model that lacked sufficient win-win qualities. The business model of a one-time, fee-for-plan was more to blame for the planner's lack of follow-up than the planner's skills. Mark's poor investment results were partly due to the fact that the planner was not the portfolio manager, the professional who actually determines which specific securities are held within the funds.

Like Mark, many investors have tried financial planning and ended up with nicely bound plans that were only partially implemented and, in many ways, were obsolete shortly after they were delivered. Or they dealt with Wall Street firms whose primary objective was to sell them more products. They even tried managing their investments themselves through discount brokerages where the costs were less but the quality and personalized nature of the advice (if any) was lacking. It's no wonder investors today have grown increasingly frustrated with the financial services industry.

Investment Management: Some Different Approaches

I personally experienced some of the same frustrations as a financial planner in the 1980s. After nine years in the industry, I once again began exploring different options.

First, I focused on investment management consulting and earned my firm's highest designation in that area. Investment management consultants are generally financial planners or they're associated with brokerage firms or independent consulting firms. They combine several style-specific investment managers (managers who invest in just one style of investments, such as growth stocks, value stocks, bonds, etc.) or mutual funds of varying styles for each of their clients. They have limited interaction and contact with these style-specific managers. Over time, the consultants attempt to switch managers to maintain an optimal blend of different styles.

There are some benefits to combining different investment management styles and managers. However, investment management consulting is not without its flaws.

- ***Few investment management consultants have ever acted as portfolio managers,*** so they're making recommendations about a discipline they've never practiced.

- *They typically base their recommendations on past performance* and correlation among the managers over too short a period of time. Unfortunately, today's best-performing style-specific managers are often the worst-performing managers in the future (because their specific styles go in and out of favor). At any rate, it takes many years to generate risk and performance data that has any meaningful statistical significance.

- *They choose style-specific institutional money managers who tend to carry many stocks.* The result: The client ends up with hundreds (and in the case of mutual funds, thousands) of individual stock positions. Since the money managers don't communicate with each other, the client gets cross-ownership (for example, three different managers buying IBM) and uncoordinated changes in asset allocation and weighting.

- *Because the money managers own so many stocks, their stock-picking ability is watered down.* Their performance tends to be highly correlated with the style or index they use as a benchmark (such as large-cap growth, mid-cap value, contrarian, etc.).

- *When a consultant changes investment managers, it's usually due to underperformance,* which normally results less from the manager's decision-making process than because his or her style has gone out of favor. Many times, by the time the manager is changed, the style comes back into favor.

- *Hiring and firing style-specific managers can be expensive.* Liquidating your entire portfolio and buying new securities from a new manager can lead to significant tax consequences and shifts in allocation. When you add all the transaction costs, the impact costs of trades in the market, the consultant's fee, and the manager's fee, you can see why it becomes difficult to receive financial value.

As a result of all these considerations, you can see why investment management consulting may not be the best model available. After several years of experience, I found that investment management consulting was not the direction in which I wanted to continue, so I next explored portfolio management. Portfolio managers generally have training or designations in the fundamentals of portfolio management, security analysis, and modern portfolio theory. The two top designations are the Chartered Market Technician (CMT) and Chartered Financial Analyst (CFA).

Typical portfolio management firms manage money in a standardized, style-specific manner. They rarely communicate directly with their clients, and they generally don't customize portfolios to meet the client's individual needs. Rather than taking this traditional approach, I became a fee-based portfolio manager in the investment management division of a large brokerage firm. My firm's business model encouraged portfolio managers to educate clients and take a customized approach. Its fee-based system, unlike the commission-based model, dramatically reduced the potential for conflicts of interest. However, my firm was not conducive to offering the kind of comprehensive advice I had in mind. The costs to the client were high compared to other options. It would require one more step before I moved to the business model I now recommend.

Personal Wealth Management: The Wave of the Future

"You did what you knew how to do,
and when you knew better, you did better."
—Maya Angelou, poet and educator

I know I added value for my clients as a stockbroker, a financial planner, an investment management consultant, and a portfolio manager. I have many friends who are highly competent advisors, and they too add value for their clients. However, many of today's investors are looking for something more.

When Aaron, a 56-year-old corporate attorney, became responsible for managing his family's $11 million fortune, he sought guidance from a tax attorney and a stockbroker. "The lawyer emphasized estate tax planning," he recalled. "He set up two charitable remainder unit trusts and a charitable lead trust. With a family limited partnership—another idea of the tax lawyer's—I found myself making choices so that the avoidance of estate taxes seemed to make my life worse instead of better. The broker showed a personal interest in me but not in any way toward furthering my goals or helping me use the money to have a better life. The money seemed like the only goal. He'd say, 'Buy bonds,' but never made any suggestions about balancing my portfolio." Aaron knew he wanted a comprehensive approach to coordinating his life issues with his personal finances. He also wanted a fee-based service, free from conflicts of interest.

To make life after 50 their best years yet, Aaron and others like him want a new kind of conversation with their advisors. They want to move to the next level, beyond portfolio management and financial planning, and work with an advisor who integrates their life vision and goals with financial coaching and customized investment management. What they're looking for can be found in a relatively new discipline called *personal wealth management.*

For many years, similar service was available only to some of the world's wealthiest families. They put together teams that combined life vision coaching with all aspects of their personal finances and portfolio management. Today, that service is becoming available to a wider audience. Personal wealth management is defined as *the pursuit and management of wealth and abundance in all their forms.*

Personal wealth involves more than money and tangible items. It's about wealth in relationships; health; knowledge; and rewarding, fulfilling experiences. If your financial wealth is not managed properly, it can create family dysfunction and unpleasant experiences. However, when managed wisely, money and tangibles are the tools you can use to create freedom and the options to pursue true wealth.

A personal wealth manager guides people through three critical areas:

- *Life vision coaching:* The rock and roll generation is beginning to understand that life after 50 includes a number of transitions—each of which affects their personal finances. A personal wealth manager can guide you through the process of creating, monitoring, and achieving your own compelling life vision, and help you make sure you'll have the money to fund it.

- *Customized investment management:* Originally, portfolio management was primarily used by institutions. It was a standardized process, where every portfolio was managed the same way. Individuals require a different level of service, focused on the issues most important to them. Customized investment management requires portfolio managers to know their clients personally and help them achieve and manage their wealth and abundance. Individuals want their portfolios customized with attention to their clearly defined *personal* risk parameters, goals, and objectives.

- *Personal financial coaching:* Many people facing life transitions want to participate in an ongoing process encompassing *all* areas of personal finance. Today more than ever, they want financial coaching from someone who can educate them about investing and personal finance to keep them from making costly mistakes; who can develop personalized strategies that are integrated with their lives; and who will monitor, review, and update those strategies to meet dynamic circumstances. Good coaches do more than advise; they draw out the best from you and work with you to create a higher level of total abundance than you ever could have imagined.

I truly believe the financial services industry will move in this direction if they follow business coach Steve Moeller's advice and move from a sales-centered to a client-centered business model and understand the connection between investments and the quality of people's lives.

A former senior vice president with one of the world's largest asset management firms has worked with the heads of the investment divisions of banks, broker-dealers, and financial planning firms. She observes, "The financial services industry would like to move more in the direction of fee-based services and personal wealth management. Many firms have made progress but continue to struggle in this area." She adds, "The current business model in the financial services industry is still based on sales and products, not on financial coaching and objective counseling. A coaching model that integrates personal finance with life issues is the wave of the future. The baby boom generation will demand a more customized and objective model from the financial services industry as their investments begin to play a more important role in their lives."

Prior to age 50, most people relate their quality of life or degree of financial freedom to their earned income. They view saving as a sacrifice. It's hard for them to make an emotional connection with their investment portfolio because it doesn't relate to their lives today; it just relates to some vague idea of the distant future. As a result of this lack of emotional connection, they generally take a left-brained, analytical approach to their investments. They base their decisions on past performance or financial presentations. Their default position is neglect and procrastination.

As the rock and roll generation begins to transition to life after 50, they become much more interested in their investments and how they can be used to impact their lives. They begin to understand that money buys financial freedom and choices. That's when it becomes essential to have a new type of discussion with their advisors, one that relates their money to their life. As rock and rollers reach this stage of life, the financial services industry will have to change to meet their demands. I believe the revolution has already begun: The financial services industry is moving along the S-curve we discussed in chapter 1, going from the standardized, one-size-fits-all model to varying degrees of customization.

As the S-curve illustrates, personal wealth management is in the innovation stage of its development cycle. Unfortunately, the term *wealth management* is undergoing some misuse. Some private bankers, brokerage firms, and financial planners have started using it to describe the same financial services they've always offered their high-net-worth clients. You've probably seen the commercials: The enthusiastically cheering advisor who gets mistaken for a parent at a child's soccer game. The teary-eyed advisor who seems like one of the family as he toasts the bride and groom. Those ads paint a picture of someone who really cares, yet the industry as a whole still hasn't embraced a model that trains and rewards advisors for delivering that level of service.

That's one reason I left the brokerage firm in which I'd practiced portfolio management and started my own firm, where my team and I utilize the seven keys to provide our high-net-worth clients with personal wealth management—that combination of life vision coaching, customized investment management, and personal financial coaching.

Key #1: Take Time to Create a Compelling Vision

Life after 50 can be your best years yet, but make no mistake: It's going to cost money. Research reported in the *Boston Globe* (June 10, 2004) indicated a 50 percent chance that one member of a healthy 65-year-old couple will live to age 92, yet few people plan to make their money last that long. According to a *Reuters* news release (June 11, 2004), Boston College economist Alicia Munnell has calculated that the typical American household approaching retirement has only $50,000 set aside. I hope you've done better than that, but obviously, the rock and roll generation as a group hasn't planned for financial freedom.

Most financial professionals would agree that their clients need some kind of a vision or blueprint for reaching their goals. However, they typically recommend benchmarking against an index such as the return on the S&P 500, or developing a spreadsheet of projections for the next 30 years. Those methods have several limitations. First, beating or failing to beat an index-related benchmark usually has little to do with whether you'll attain financial freedom for the rest of your life. Second, trying to beat a benchmark often causes you to take too much risk. Finally, benchmarking can be extremely disempowering. By delegating investment management to your advisor and measuring against unpredictable indices or long-term projections, you have no real control over the outcome.

To make life after 50 your best years yet, you need an empowering process that's relevant to your interests and goals. Like building a house, the goal of becoming financially secure must begin with a vision. If you wanted to build your dream house, where would you start? Would you run right out and buy the lumber? Of course not. You'd first spend time thinking and dreaming about your house. What would it look like? Where would it be? You'd probably look at other houses to get some good ideas, then you'd find an architect to draw up the plans.

In the same way, personal wealth managers use a wealth management benchmarking process to help people clarify their vision and avoid unforced errors—those unseen obstacles that can derail their financial train but are easily prevented with a little advance planning. People often worry that they've left something undone. Maybe their wills aren't up to date, or their investments have too much risk or aren't in balance. The world is unpredictable—emergencies arise, markets go down, accidents happen.

To help our clients, my firm has developed the Wealth Management Benchmark®, a process that helps them clarify their vision and measure their progress against their own goals in each of six wealth management categories. It's designed to direct clients toward right-brain visioning rather than left-brain statistics.

Although we generally use a much more extensive computerized version and coach each client through the process, I'm including an abbreviated form just to give you a taste.

The Wealth Management Benchmark

In the following exercise, you'll find six categories or critical life areas, with four statements under each one. For each statement, you'll be asked to do three things:

1. ***Determine the issue's importance.*** If it's important to you, place a check mark in the first column. If the issue is not important, leave the column blank.

2. ***Determine the issue's completeness.*** If the issue is incomplete and needs your attention, place a check mark in the second column If the issue has been completed, leave the column blank.

3. ***Determine a time frame for completion.*** If you placed check marks in the first and second columns (meaning the issue is important and needs to be completed), insert a completion time in the third column. Write "3" if you want to complete it in the next 3 months, "6" if you want to complete it within 4 to 6 months, and "12" if you intend to complete it within the next 7 to 12 months.

Let's go through the first issue together. It says, "Create a compelling vision of your future life." Would doing that be important to you? Do you think it would be a good idea to spend some time developing a compelling vision for your future? If so, place a check mark in the first column.

Next, what's your level of completeness in this issue? Let's say you've thought about it a little but you really haven't gone as far as you'd like. In that case, place a check mark in the second column.

Finally, what's your time frame for completion? Let's say you'd be willing to do it within the next 6 months, but you're really busy right now and know it will be at least 4 months before you'll have the time. In that case, write "6" in the last column.

Go ahead and complete the exercise, and then we'll take the final steps.

	Importance	Needs Completion	Timing 3 (1–3 mos.) 6 (4–6 mos.) 12 (7–12 mos.)
Quality of Life Index™			
1. Create a compelling vision of your future life.			
2. Create your BHAG (big hairy audacious goal) and a process for achieving it.			
3. Calculate your "real age" on www.realage.com.			
4. Take the steps recommended by your physician (and/or www.realage.com) to enhance your longevity.			
Net Worth & Cash Management			
1. Create a net worth and cash flow statement.			
2. Establish a method to track your cash flow and expenses (e.g., Quicken or Microsoft Money).			
3. Confirm that any existing debt is tax efficient and represents a reasonable percentage of your assets.			
4. Confirm that all tax-advantaged employee benefits [e.g., 401(k), deferred compensation] are being maximized.			
Investment Planning			
1. Discuss your overall investment philosophy and create an investment policy statement (IPS).			
2. Confirm diversification among and within different investment classes.			

3. Confirm that you own the highest quality securities.			
4. Ensure that all your financial assets are following the directives of your IPS.			
Retirement Planning			
1. Explore the possibilities of continued employment or other sources for generating income.			
2. Determine tax-advantaged portfolio withdrawals to meet your cash needs.			
3. Create a process for generating cash flow at retirement.			
4. Complete a retirement planning analysis.			
Estate & Legacy Planning			
1. Discuss your estate and legacy philosophy with an estate planning advisor.			
2. Create a detailed outline of your objectives.			
3. Establish trusts and draft wills and all necessary related documents.			
4. With family members, discuss life support, final wishes, and other decisions to be made if you were to become incapacitated.			
Asset & Income Protection			
1. Discuss your insurance philosophy with your insurance advisor.			
2. Identify the amount of insurance necessary to meet your family's needs in the event of an untimely death and develop a life insurance plan.			
3. Confirm that your insurance (auto, property, casualty, personal liability, etc.) is appropriate and cost effective.			
4. Analyze and make decisions regarding long-term care.			

Now look at the timing column. On a separate sheet of paper, list the issues to which you assigned a time frame, in order of priority. In other words, start with all the "3" issues, then all the "6" issues, and finally all the "12" issues. The result will be your action plan. Post this list where you can see it often, and commit to meeting the deadlines you've set. Then, you can work with your advisors to tackle each issue, determine an optimum schedule for reviewing and evaluating your progress, and establish the best ways to continue fine-tuning your individualized personal wealth management strategy.

Before you leave this exercise, choose two items from your action plan and commit to a date for getting them done. By taking this simple step, you'll be well on your way to achieving your vision of financial wealth and abundance.

Please remember, this exercise is offered just to give you a taste of the experience. The actual Wealth Management Benchmark is much more extensive, and coaching and counseling are important parts of the process.

Key #2: Connect Your Vision to Your Values, Passion, and Purpose

By completing the sample Wealth Management Benchmark, you've begun the process of creating a vision of the goals you want to achieve. Unlike traditional financial planning, where the advisor decides which areas are important, the Wealth Management Benchmark lets you determine each issue's importance and its current level of completion—based on your values.

Two years ago, at age 60, Sid retired from his position as CEO of a manufacturing company. Although he missed the social contact that went along with the job, he looked forward to taking some time off to recover from a bad case of burnout and reinvent himself. "When I retired," Sid recalled, "I determined in my mind that after a long, successful, grinding, high-pressure kind of an environment, I really wanted something more gratifying and on a different level."

One of the first things Sid did was to complete the values process described in chapter 3 and the Wealth Management Benchmark to clarify his priorities. His top four values painted an accurate picture of this hard-driving, adventurous man: his list included self-renewal, taste (which he defined as always wanting to taste new things), freedom, and courage.

True to his values and financial priorities, retired life didn't hold Sid's interest for long. "People would say, 'What do you do?' and I'd say, 'I don't do anything,'" he recalled. "Finally one day I said, 'Gosh, I'm concerned with the fact that people are embarrassing me because I'm not doing anything, and they're telling me I'm kind of wrong in that. Second, I'm frustrated with this economic environment, with my assets not working for me. And third, I'm getting listless.' That was my evolution after I'd had a sabbatical."

After reviewing his values and wealth management goals, Sid decided to start his own business. He chose to use some of his savings to invest in himself. He did a little visioning and came up with a plan. Sort of.

"I know how much money I want to invest," he said. "I know generally what location I want to do it in, I know how many employees I do or don't want. I know what the requirements for additional capitalization might be. I know the cash flow and I know what kind of return on my investment I want out of that. Now, let's go find something that I can do." Though it might not sound like it, Sid was practicing one of the most important lessons this book has to offer: *First the vision, then the plan.* He knew how he wanted his life to work. The details would fill themselves in later on.

Today, Sid's one of the happiest people I know. Although he puts in long hours at his new car wash, he doesn't show a single trace of burnout these days. "I'm happy because all of these elements have fallen together," he reports. "The fact that I'm a car wash attendant (I say humorously) is okay with me. In fact, if I socialize and somebody asks, 'What do you do?' I say, 'I'm a car wash attendant.' I have no problem with that at all. You have to find satisfaction wherever it may lead you."

Like Sid, you now have the tools to help you create a compelling vision and connect it to your values, passion, or purpose. How will you use these tools to create total abundance in your life?

Key #3: Educate Yourself and Find a Great Coach

This section, of necessity, will deal with technical topics that may seem to be more than you want to know about the mechanics of investing. However, if you want to build a successful portfolio, you need to educate yourself about the basics. The purpose of this information is not to teach you how to be a portfolio manager but to teach you the fundamentals of a rules-based portfolio management process. (More details will come in a future book dedicated exclusively to investing.)

Without a proven, well-thought-out system to follow, people often find themselves making decisions based on emotions of fear and greed. To have an achievable vision of financial security, you need a disciplined, rules-based approach to constructing and managing your portfolio. Once you understand the rules and the process, you'll be able to confidently use them or choose a portfolio manager who does. You'll be able to sleep at night, secure in the knowledge that you or your portfolio manager are doing everything possible to bring you financial security, regardless of what the market, other investors, and other financial advisors may do.

My years of experience indicate that the best portfolio management style is based on four commonsense rules. They work well for most people, even though their financial goals are diverse.

1. Understand risk and make it work for you. If you can't control the risk in your portfolio, you can't control the outcome.

2. Get well diversified and stay that way all your life.

3. Don't let the emotions of fear and greed drive your investment process.

4. Develop and follow an investment policy statement.

Rule 1: Understand Risk and Make It Work for You

Occasionally, one of my clients asks me to buy safe or "risk-free" investments. Unfortunately, I can't comply with that request, because there's no such thing as a risk-free investment. Once you know a little about risk, you'll understand why.

People usually define *risk* as the likelihood that the value of an investment could fluctuate in price or, in some cases, lose money. However, this is only one type of risk, the type called *market risk*. Unfortunately, there are several types of investment risk, and they all affect the return on your investment in some way.

A broader definition of risk includes the following:

- *Market risk* includes loss of principal, fluctuations in investment price, and lack of liquidity (the inability to sell an investment when you want to). If market risk were the only type of risk you needed to worry about, it would make sense to invest only in certificates of deposit, U.S. Treasury bills, and money markets because they're not subject to market risk. Unfortunately, they are subject to other types of risk.

- *Inflation risk* is the loss of purchasing power over a period of time; it forces you to spend more money over time to maintain the lifestyle to which you are accustomed. Your personal inflation rate may be higher than the government-quoted rate, based on how you spend your money. Most people will agree that it costs much more to live today than it did 10 or 15 years ago.

- *Tax risk* is the impact of investment taxes on investment return. For example, if investment income is taxable, individuals in the highest tax bracket will lose a significant percentage of the total income earned on their investments. In addition, they'll have to pay capital gains tax on realized gains when the investments are sold.

- *Reinvestment risk* occurs when the proceeds from maturing securities like bonds may not be reinvested at the same rate at which they were initially invested. For example, most investors profited from the 20 percent-plus returns of the stock market from 1995 through 1999. The history of the market indicates that returns will most likely be less in the future. Retirees who locked in high interest rates on bonds in the late '90s will only be able to renew those bonds at about half of the original interest rate.

- *Opportunity risk* occurs when people miss a chance to take a path that could lead to higher net worth. For example, by overestimating their need for readily available cash, they may miss the opportunity to invest in something that could have generated higher returns.

- *Psychological risk* is associated with the feelings of fear and greed. Many people tend to get too optimistic (greedy) when markets go up; they put too large of a percentage of their assets in risky investments when times are good. On the other hand, when markets decline, people experience fear, which causes them to pull money out at the bottom of the market. Since people generally feel bad at the bottom and good at the top, an emotion-based investment process is doomed from the start. People who practice this method tend to have limited success investing over the long term.

- *Procrastination risk* reflects the lost opportunity that results from not taking action at the proper time. Because of uncertainty about which action to take, procrastinators simply avoid making decisions and do nothing. Procrastination also occurs when you fail to recognize the importance of taking immediate action.

Once you understand the different types of risk, you'll understand why there's no such thing as a risk-free investment. Simply put, there's a relationship between risk and return. Taking no risks leads to receiving no real returns. Taking on more risk can result in higher returns as well as a higher possibility for losses. In fact, investing in a portfolio of high-risk securities can lead to high negative returns. This happens because risky securities tend to fluctuate more, resulting in a large loss when the securities fall out of favor. Such a loss can be so great that the investor cannot recover and recoup the losses.

Now that you understand risk, how can you make it work for you? The answer is surprisingly simple: Add time and diversify your holdings.

Rule 2: Get Well Diversified and Stay That Way All Your Life

You've already learned that, for a single investment class (such as stocks or real estate), more risk generally leads to a greater return. Is there any way to alter the risk-return equation and get higher return while taking lower risk? Nobel Prize winner Harry Markowitz, the father of modern portfolio theory, says yes.

More than 50 years ago, before the widespread use of computers, Markowitz observed that you can reduce a portfolio's volatility by combining investments with different patterns of return. In *Asset Allocation* (McGraw-Hill, 2000), author Roger C. Gibson explains Markowitz's approach:

Before modern portfolio theory, investment management was a two-dimensional process focusing primarily on the volatility and return characteristics of individual securities. As a result of Harry Markowitz's work, recognition grew regarding the importance of the interrelationships among securities within portfolios. Modern portfolio theory added a third dimension to portfolio management that evaluates a security's *diversification effect* on a portfolio. This term refers to the impact that the inclusion of a particular asset class or security will have on the volatility and return characteristics of the overall portfolio.

Modern portfolio theory thus shifted the focus of attention away from individual securities and toward a consideration of the portfolio as a whole.

To summarize, modern portfolio theory says you can generate a higher return with lower risk—if the investments in your portfolio work together. One of the basics behind this theory is the attempt to create an *efficient portfolio,* one that earns the highest return with the least amount of volatility. This can be accomplished by owning a diverse group of securities that fluctuate in different ways.

Let's consider an example. An oil company's stock and a transportation company's stock will generally move in opposite directions as a result of shared economic circumstances. If oil prices go up, it's usually good for the oil company but bad for the transportation company. Both companies' stocks may be good long-term investments, but in the short term one should underperform.

A better scenario is to invest in stocks that move up and down independently. For instance, the stock price of a manufacturing company in Indianapolis probably wouldn't be impacted by the same market conditions that affect the stock price of a company that owns 20 fast-food restaurants in Hong Kong. Both stocks could go up or down at the same time, but not because there's a relationship between the two. With a portfolio of unrelated securities, you can make more money with less risk during volatile market fluctuations.

Let me give you a simple example of how market volatility can work for you. The following figure shows two portfolios, owned by two different investors.

Investor A, seeking maximum return, concentrates his securities in stocks that have similar characteristics (Portfolio A). Investor B wants to spread the risk, so she buys a diversified mix of securities from different investment classes, such as domestic stocks, bonds, international securities, or real estate (Portfolio B). Each portfolio is originally worth $100.

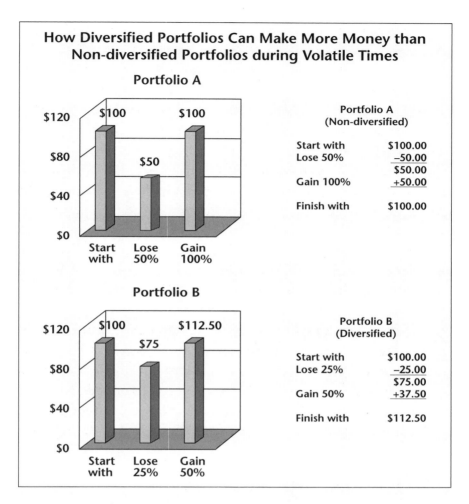

Suppose these portfolios experience a bear market, which is defined as a market in which prices drop or "correct" by 20 percent or more. The top graph in the figure shows that, during the bear market, Portfolio A loses 50 percent of its value. That kind of sharp loss can easily occur in a portfolio that has very little diversification. Investor A is left with just $50, meaning he'll have to make a 100 percent gain in the future just to be back where he started.

The lower graph shows what happens to Portfolio B during the bear market. Again, Investor B starts with a $100 investment. However, since her portfolio is diversified among different industries and types of securities, it's only half as volatile as Portfolio A.

Thus, the bear market causes Portfolio B to drop only 25 percent (half as much as Portfolio A), leaving Investor B with $75.

Eventually the market rises again, sending Portfolio A up 100 percent to recoup the original loss, and sending Portfolio B up by 50 percent ($37.50)—only half as much as Portfolio A, because of the greater diversity. However, Investor B now has $112.50 in her portfolio.

As strange as it may sound, the risk that most people are afraid of—market volatility—can actually help enhance your return. Portfolio B made more money than Portfolio A because B dropped less when the market went down. It also went up less when the market rose, but ended up with a higher return because the advance occurred from a bigger base ($75 instead of $50). I call this the ratchet effect: The more volatile the market, the more the diversified portfolio's return is enhanced.

This is a very simple example of how modern portfolio theory works. Remember, you don't have to take more risk to make more money. One of the goals of the diversified portfolio is to benefit from volatility and achieve more consistent returns than typical stock or bond indices. Having more consistent returns makes it possible to make more money over time with less risk.

Rule 3: Don't Let Emotions Drive Your Investment Process

When you wake up one morning and realize that your portfolio's value has dropped, your emotions tell you to sell. If you do, your losses become permanent and you won't be in the market when it goes back up. That's what happens when you surrender to psychological risk and let your emotions replace a strong investment discipline.

I firmly believe that the biggest risk people face in managing their investments comes from their emotions. Money tends to be an emotional subject. It may seem easy today to say you're investing for long-term results. However, it may not be so easy tomorrow if the Dow Jones Industrial Average drops 500 points, or the market moves downward by 10 percent or more, or if rising interest rates cause bonds to decline.

To make matters worse, you'll be constantly bombarded by news stories on the current state of the market. Most of this financial analysis will be short-term oriented. For example, if the market is down one day, the media will likely say the Dow "plunged" and offer three or four reasons why it happened. When the market is up, the media will interview experts who give specific advice on how to thrive in current market conditions, especially recommending stocks that are doing well at the moment. In short, the media focuses primarily on what's happening now, instead of trying to teach people how to follow a disciplined investment style.

There'll always be people with a narrowly focused investment strategy who happen to be in the right place at the right time. They'll be making huge returns today, and they'll always be covered by the media. If you listen to their advice, you'll be chasing the hot manager or fund after it's already gone up; more often than not, you'll be buying at the top. What you won't hear is that, ultimately, investments that have the highest returns will also have the greatest losses. Proper portfolio management is about consistency in returns and managing risk.

My advice is simple: Don't get your financial advice from the media. News articles that engender feelings of fear or greed often lead to portfolio adjustments that seem satisfying in the short term but may have negative consequences in the future. By the time information reaches the media, it's already been reflected in the market.

Here are three more points to help you keep emotion out of your investment decisions:

- ***The best defense against emotional investing is knowledge.*** You don't need to become an expert at portfolio management and the stock and bond markets, but it's important to learn the fundamentals and adopt a rules-based system for investment management. Once you have a process that meets your objectives, make only small adjustments, even if the process is currently out of favor.

- ***When short-term results are disappointing, don't panic.*** Remember that a well-diversified portfolio fluctuates over time, so declines are generally temporary and should eventually turn into gains. A diversified portfolio has the virtue of consistency, losing a little today, gaining a little tomorrow—one step back, two steps forward. Over time, by avoiding the extremes, such a portfolio will always achieve the best investment results.

- ***Have the discipline to stay focused on long-term success.*** As the old saying goes, if it ain't broke, don't fix it. Don't worry too much about the month-to-month fluctuations in your portfolio value. Over the long term, a diversified portfolio will grow at a fairly consistent rate with a minimum of risk.

Rule 4: Develop and Follow an Investment Policy Statement

An investment policy statement outlines the investment guidelines and procedures to be followed by the portfolio manager. It clarifies the appropriate investment process so you and your portfolio manager know you're on the same page. It identifies your needs, goals, objectives, and risk tolerances, and it establishes reasonable expectations, objectives, and guidelines for investing the portfolio's assets. It defines the responsibilities of investor and advisor, and it encourages effective communication between you and your portfolio manager.

A well-written investment policy statement increases the likelihood that your portfolio will continue to meet your financial needs. Perhaps most important, the investment policy statement clarifies the relationship between your money and the freedom to do what you want.

We'll go into further detail about creating and following an investment policy statement in key #4.

Manage Your Own Portfolio or Seek Professional Help?

By now, you may begin to realize that managing a substantial portfolio is a complex and time-consuming endeavor. In fact, if you learned everything in this chapter about the basics of investing, you'd only begin to scratch the surface of the knowledge you'd need to successfully manage your own investments. So, the question arises: Should you try to manage your own portfolio or hire a trained professional?

You might think I'd have only one answer for this, since I make my living as a portfolio manager and personal wealth manager. However, in reality, I can't answer this question for you. There's really no right or wrong answer; it depends on your personal style.

- Are you a hands-on type who likes to personally oversee every aspect of your personal finances and investments? Are you fascinated with the complexities of the financial markets? Do you consider security analysis and portfolio management to be an enjoyable, productive endeavor? If so, you'll probably be willing to manage your portfolio on your own.

- On the other hand, do you consider investment management a burden? Do you want to understand your portfolio management process, but not necessarily handle its day-to-day maintenance? Are you comfortable delegating investment decisions to an advisor? If so, you may want to consider working with a professional.

Before you decide, you'll want to interview several financial advisors and ask your friends who've worked with these professionals. Larry and Lindsay, a couple in their 50s, were searching for a financial advisor. Through the Financial Planning Association (www.fpanet.org), they obtained a list of about 30 local financial planners, including me. They sent each one a letter saying that Larry would be taking early retirement and asking how the financial planner could help. In reply, I sent Larry some information on my process for working with clients.

Several months later, Larry called me and arranged a meeting. By the time they came to my office, Larry and Lindsay had previously met with several potential advisors. They presented an organized picture of their financial situation and were loaded with questions. We talked about what they wanted in an advisory relationship and the types of clients with whom I'd successfully worked in the past. After a series of meetings over the next few weeks, we decided to work together. As an added benefit, we've also become good friends.

Larry and Lindsay used an intelligent approach to finding a financial advisor. "You have to educate yourself," Larry suggested. "You have to know what you're going after, and the only way to do that is to talk with people, find out what their philosophy is, and find out if you agree with that philosophy. We discounted certain people right away because their personalities didn't mesh with ours."

Here's an example of an advisor search process:

- If you don't already know an advisor, you might want to begin with an Internet search. Go to Google or your favorite search engine and input "personal wealth manager," "financial planner," "portfolio manager," or similar terms, and your nearest city.

- Choose several candidates who seem to have an approach and business model you can relate to. Send each a letter or e-mail stating your intentions and requesting information.

- Schedule appointments and interview each candidate.

Here are some points to consider as you interview potential advisors.

Although *credentials* don't necessarily guarantee you're getting a great advisor, they provide a starting point and show that the advisor has gone through training, taken a certification exam, and focused on a subject for a certain period of time. Anyone can call themselves a financial advisor; look for recognized designations such as Certified Financial Planner (CFP), Chartered Market Technician (CMT), Chartered Retirement Planning Counselor (CRPC), Certified Investment Management Consultant (CIMC), and Chartered Financial Analyst (CFA). Keep in mind that each of these designations is specialized; you might want to look for an advisor with multiple credentials.

In many industries, youth and fresh ideas are great. In this business, there's no substitute for years of *experience.* Diversity of experience is also important. Make sure your potential advisor has a good understanding of all aspects of personal finance as well as portfolio management.

Referrals can be helpful, but remember, someone else's objectives may not be the same as yours, and their opinions of an advisor will reflect their own experience. Be wary of letters of recommendation; the advisor certainly wouldn't show you a negative letter, and nearly everyone has some satisfied clients. If you do receive a referral, follow up with specific, open-ended questions, such as, What did the advisor do for you? What did you like about him or her? Use negative references to weed out less-experienced or poor advisors; if someone says, "They took all my money and I never heard from them again," run!

Visit a potential advisor's *Web site* to get a feel for his or her personality and approach. Obviously, Web sites are a lot like advertising, because the advisor controls the content, but you can use them to gather preliminary information (such as credentials and experience) and get a general overview of the advisor's philosophy.

Your relationship with a financial advisor is a long-term commitment and requires a bond of mutual trust and candor. Make sure there's a *good personal connection.* Also make sure your advisor is a good coach and is interested in helping you clarify and obtain your objectives. A good coach is also a good teacher. That's important, because the more you know, the more likely you are to stick with your discipline.

Potential advisors should be able to explain their *risk management strategy.* Make sure a potential advisor can quantify and manage the volatility of your portfolio in a way you can understand. What's the highest and lowest volatility (risk range) it can have? Don't put a lot of credence in past returns; every money manager I know seems to have charts and graphs that place them as one of the top money managers of all time. Since we know the majority of money managers don't beat the market, how can everyone you talk to be one of the best? Focus more on their process and discipline and how it can potentially fit your needs.

Make sure potential advisors have a *money management strategy.* What do I mean by money management? Here's a simple analogy. I don't know very much about playing cards, but even the best blackjack player with a great card-counting system might only be able to win 60 out of 100 hands. The key to whether he'd make money at the end of the night has to do with the way he manages his money. The same is true when it comes to investing. You could buy more winners than losers, but without a good money management strategy, you'd still end up losing.

Make sure you're comfortable with the potential advisor's *fee structure* before you hire him or her. In the commission-based model, the advisor tends to be more focused on creating transactions. Because of the business model, a fee-only advisor is more likely to give objective advice than someone who's commission-based. Most fees are based on assets; the advisor makes more money when the portfolio goes up and less when it goes down. Obviously, a fee-based advisor wants to make you money and keep you happy for the long term. If you become dissatisfied and leave, the advisor no longer collects the management fee. However, remember that even some fee-based advisors benefit directly from commissions or indirectly from "soft dollars" (credits rebated to advisors from brokerages in the form of research, hardware, software, terminals, and the like). Be sure to ask if the potential advisor benefits from trading or anything other than a management fee.

Find someone with *quarterback ability.* If you choose to go through the personal wealth management process, you'll work with professionals in a variety of areas (life vision coaching, tax planning, portfolio management, etc.). For the most part, they'll be reacting to issues that arise from the two dynamic parts of your wealth: your life decisions and your investments. Your life decisions have a huge impact on your personal financial condition. Your choices about how much you spend or save, your career, and your lifestyle are dynamic and have a ripple effect. Investment decisions made by the portfolio manager also affect most areas of your personal finances (such as your liquidity, tax situation, long-term investment success, estate plan, and many other financial and life issues). That's why portfolio managers are well positioned to act as personal wealth managers and are an intricate part of your entire team. Personal wealth managers should have good general knowledge in each area and be able to identify estate, tax, and other issues that inevitably arise. They should have a strong coaching background and be able to act as your personal coach to help you identify your goals and create a plan to achieve them. Finally, they should have a life vision coach on staff and connections with experts in the various wealth management fields.

Key #4: Formulate and Implement a Measurable Plan

Setting clear investment objectives can be a real challenge for most investors. A number of factors determine a portfolio's success or failure:

- *Risk tolerance:* People often describe themselves as conservative or moderate, but what does that mean? In truth, most people have no idea of the risk level inherent in their portfolios at any given time.

- *Expectations:* The bull market of the late 1990s caused investors to feel overly confident and they became too aggressive.

- *Market exposure:* The subsequent bear market of the early 2000s caused many investors to lighten their exposure to risk and withdraw from the market after it had already gone down. Having too much exposure when markets go down and not enough when markets go up is one of the primary reasons people have poor investment experiences.

To make life after 50 your best years yet, you need a clearly articulated plan for how your money should be invested. As you learned earlier, an investment policy statement (IPS) outlines the investment guidelines and procedures to be followed by your portfolio manager.

Creating an IPS compels you to put your investment strategy in writing and commit to a disciplined investment plan. An IPS is like a blueprint and report card, rolled into one. It lets you and your advisor protect your portfolio from impromptu revisions of sound long-term policy. It helps you maintain a long-term focus when short-term market events may distress you and even cause you to question your policy. With the objective, predetermined plan outlined in your investment policy statement, you avoid emotional decision making and concentrate on your rules-based plan. A well-written IPS increases the likelihood that your portfolio will continue to meet your financial needs. Perhaps most important, the IPS clarifies the relationship between your money and your freedom to do what you want.

Your investment policy statement should include the following components:

- *Investment objectives:* A written paragraph or two about your vision for your money. What's important about the money to you? What's the purpose? How can it be used to bring about rewarding and fulfilling opportunities?

- *Risk guidelines:* These quantify the level of risk you're comfortable with. (Again, discuss with your advisor how he or she quantifies risk.)

- *Asset allocation guidelines:* Asset allocation refers to your portfolio's blend of stocks, bonds, and cash equivalents. Finding the best asset mix is crucial if you want to meet your goals. A balanced portfolio has an appropriate mix of stocks, bonds, and cash equivalents at all times and is designed to meet the agreed-upon risk targets. Your asset allocation should change over time based on market volatility and outlook.

- *Diversification guidelines:* Your advisor should have a process to help measure the percentage benefit of diversification, and a method to identify your portfolio's volatility.

- *Tax considerations:* Are there any special tax considerations for your portfolio? For example, do you have low-cost-basis stocks or a large tax loss to carry forward? For taxable portfolios, the manager should focus on harvesting short-term tax losses and pursuing long-term capital gains.

- *Action plan:* List the important financial issues that need to be addressed. Your action plan should include a process that assures timely implementation (this can be generated by completing and periodically updating the wealth management benchmarking process). Action plan items should be reviewed during your meetings with your advisor.

Unlike those books of projections that never come true, an investment policy statement puts your investment strategy in writing and shows the disciplined investment plan upon which you and your advisor agree.

Key #5: Monitor Your Progress and Update the Plan as Needed

One of the most important factors in building net worth is to think about and focus on some aspect of building net worth every day. This thought process changes your *goal* of financial security to a *vision* of financial security. It also increases the probability that your vision will actually happen.

Do you remember Fred, the airline pilot from chapter 2? A key ingredient to his success was focusing his attention on building net worth. He used net worth and cash flow statements to monitor his ongoing progress and see how he was spending his money. He also set specific goals and updated them as he accomplished each one. Follow Fred's example and be mindful of your spending. You don't necessarily need to cut back, but be aware that money gets lost when you fail to think about cost-versus-benefit issues.

Another important tool for monitoring your progress is meeting periodically with your advisor to discuss the strategy and process for attaining your goals. If something doesn't look right, ask questions. Confirm that the agreed-upon investment process is being followed. If it is, then focus on the future and the areas you can control. What are you going to do next? If the markets are acting a certain way, what's your plan for moving forward? Focus on actions that will add value. If that requires additional education or steps you should take, make the appropriate adjustments.

Monitor Your Long-Term Progress, Not the Daily News

Some people think monitoring their progress means watching their investments go up and down every day. Believe me, there's absolutely no value in doing that.

The official scorer for the Indiana Pacers is a friend of mine. Sometimes at halftime, I go down to the scorer's table and he gives me the official stats from the first half of the game, much to the envy of all the guys around me. We study the stats, commenting on how forward Jermaine O'Neal should have taken more shots or how shooting guard Reggie Miller carried the first half by hitting four out of five three-pointers.

We can analyze the stats all night, but will it impact the second half of the game? Of course not. We can watch the game, get emotional, and yell as much as we want (which is fun at a game), or we can sit there and have zero reaction. Neither approach has any impact on the game, except maybe if the team is playing at home and gets inspired by our cheers.

As for the team, when the whistle blows, they do the best they can, making decisions based on their discipline and probabilities. Although they don't win every game, the Pacers' basketball style or discipline has worked well throughout the season. They make slight adjustments to their game plan based on how they match up against each opponent. Assuming that they have a solid rules-based philosophy, they'd be foolish to totally change their style or get rid of their core players or coaches from one game to the next.

Just like the Pacers, your portfolio's results won't be affected by whether you watch it go up and down every day. The key is to develop and follow a rules-based philosophy that works, make adjustments based on your personal needs or market conditions, and most important, stick with your process for the long term.

The Crowd Is Generally Wrong

Here's another mistake frequently made in the interest of monitoring. Instead of understanding the fundamentals of portfolio management and the rules for smart investing, many people look to "the crowd" for investment advice. When the crowd agrees that the market's going up, they jump in. When the crowd thinks the market's going down, they're ready to jump out. Unfortunately, the crowd is almost always wrong. Markets tend to move opposite what the majority of people think.

By the time everyone believes the market is going up, most people have invested as much as they're comfortable investing; there are no buyers left to support the market's upward movement. That causes the market's trend to stall, and a new countertrend begins as the selling starts. As people with high expectations start losing money, crowd psychology takes over again.

The stronger your gut feeling is, the more likely you are to be wrong. Bull markets "crawl a wall of worry"—when people are the most worried, the market is nearing the bottom. But when the crowd agrees that "We're in the new paradigm" and "It's different this time," it's a sign that you've just experienced a boom or a bust, depending on which way the market's been moving.

Crowd psychology occurs at extreme valuations of the market, both high and low. Sharp advances bring about sharp declines, and vice versa. In reality, the crowd tends to be correct in the middle part of a trend but wrong at the major turning points, where much of the money is made or lost.

In late March 2003, after three years of the worst bear market in our generation's memory, people were pessimistic. The United States had just invaded Iraq, and oilfields could be blown up at any moment, throwing our already slow economy into a panic. Conventional thinking expected the market to drop. However, from that time until the peak in the first quarter of 2004, the Dow Jones Industrial Average rose from 7,500 to 10,600. In fact, most of the market's rise occurred while our country was on the highest terror alert.

Rather than listening to crowd psychology and constantly changing your investment policies, you're much safer with a rules-based process for managing your money, a system that helps limit emotional reactions to major events. Even though market returns may be erratic in the short term, remember that they're fairly predictable over a longer period of time and stay in for the long term. Even if you're over 50 years old, you have plenty of time to ride out market cycles. With proper diversification, the peaks and valleys can be dramatically reduced.

Don't let market volatility force you into rash decisions. Following the crowd psychology, with its basis in the human emotions of fear and greed, can wreak havoc on your long-term investment program and prevent you from making your second 50 years the best years yet. Don't fall into the traps of buying high and selling low. Remember that major shifts in asset allocation can destroy a long-term investment program, and follow a rules-based portfolio management system, a process you can believe in. Once your system is in place, sit back, relax, and leave the crowd mentality to the uninformed.

Key #6: Enjoy Your Abundance

"Prosperity is only an instrument to be used,
not a deity to be worshiped."
—Calvin Coolidge, 30th U.S. president

For most people, the issue of finances usually hovers somewhere in the back of their minds. It's an area they're always a little uneasy about, like waiting for the other shoe to drop. They aren't sure they've done the right thing. They tend to lack knowledge in many areas of personal finance, don't know what they should know, and in many cases, have neglected to do anything at all. If they haven't formulated a plan and something unexpected comes up—like they want to take an exotic vacation or do something extravagant and out of the norm—they tell themselves, "I don't know if I should spend that money. Maybe it's not a good idea." Raised by depression-era parents, they feel guilty about enjoying and using their money instead of saving it.

Personal wealth management takes the opposite approach. If you do your homework and take time to work through the keys described in this book, you'll have the peace of mind that comes from knowing you've addressed every issue that's important to you. You'll continue to monitor your progress, but that's different from waiting, watching, and worrying. You'll know that money and tangibles can be used as tools to help create enjoyable and rewarding experiences, and you'll be free to enjoy your abundance.

Some financial advisors will tell you, "Find some other way to get the money. Don't touch your investments." Obviously, I'm not suggesting that you spend all your money for fun and fail to save for the future. However, investing in yourself is one of the best investments you can make.

Vince, a 63-year-old client of mine, had worked for the same company for several years. When he was offered the opportunity to buy the company, he jumped at the chance. "I elected to take some of my retirement money and invest it in myself and my own company," he said. "I didn't want to retire, I don't want to retire, and I probably never will retire." Vince plans to leave the company to his children and heirs someday, but right now he's having the time of his life running it himself.

Life after 50 can be a time to start thinking about enjoying some of the money you've saved. Maybe you're planning to retire and live from accumulated income. Maybe you'd like to stop working 50 or 60 hours a week and enjoy more time for your personal life. Maybe you'd like to have a year or two off to take a sabbatical, go back to school, or start a new business. If so, you'll want to talk to your advisor about the most efficient ways to use your investments to supplement your financial needs.

Clients frequently ask whether they should shift their investment objective from growth to income when they want to start tapping into their investments. I believe your relative need for growth versus income remains unchanged over the years. Indeed, the people who shift their portfolios to produce more income assume greater inflation and reinvestment risk.

Contrary to popular belief, you shouldn't shift your portfolio to overweighting income-producing investments when you begin to tap your nest egg. Making a radical change in your portfolio to concentrate on one investment class (fixed income) is a big mistake. The diversified portfolio is the most conservative when it comes to protecting you against all the risks mentioned at the beginning of this chapter. A portfolio invested only in income-producing investments is not diversified and is subject to inflation, taxes, and increases in interest rates that will cause your funds to decline. A good financial advisor can construct a cash management system that will produce enough liquidity to meet your cash needs without destroying the diversification in your portfolio. With a rules-based system and an efficient strategy for tapping into your investments, you'll be free to enjoy the abundance you've worked so hard to attain.

Key #7: Leave a Lasting Legacy

If you work hard, invest wisely, and follow the strategies outlined in this book, the probabilities are very high that you'll have money, financial assets, and hard assets left over at the end of your life. What will happen to everything you've accumulated? That's a question only you can answer.

Too often, people neglect to develop a strategy for their assets, and their loved ones end up bearing the burden. I'm sure you've seen families where relatives wound up feuding over who inherited what. With no processes or procedures in place, decisions like those must be made at a time when people are emotionally vulnerable.

I know it's no one's favorite topic, but managing your wealth includes thinking about those issues. What do you want to have happen with your assets? What kind of legacy do you want to leave? Do you want to use your wealth to make the world better? College campuses are filled with libraries and facilities funded by people who wanted to leave a legacy. Do you want to honor someone who had a lasting impact on your life by funding a scholarship or starting a foundation in their name? Your wealth will continue long after you're gone. What do you want it to do on your behalf?

It may help to think about the negative events that could occur if you procrastinate long enough. Think about your kids. What do you think would happen if you left $3 million to a 25-year-old? Maybe you need to do some estate planning or set up some trust funds. That's another great thing about completing the Wealth Management Benchmark or other similar process—they remind you to focus on areas of life you may have neglected until now.

A client once told me, "My estate plan is I think I'll live forever, and so far it's working." I hope that's not your estate planning philosophy. Remember the old saying: If you fail to plan, you're planning to fail. This chapter has offered some exciting new tools for creating and planning for financial abundance. I encourage you to take advantage of them and plan to make life after 50 your most financially abundant years yet!

Before you leave this chapter, please take a few moments to review the coaching questions. Then we'll wrap things up with a look at what the future holds for the rock and roll generation.

◆　◆　◆

Coaching Questions

Are You Serious About Your Money?

- Life after 50 can be your best years yet, but make no mistake: It's going to cost money.

    Have you saved enough money to maintain your current lifestyle? Do you have a rules-based plan in place for attaining financial freedom?

- The Wealth Management Benchmark was designed to help you avoid unforced errors.

    Did you complete the sample exercise in this chapter? If not, please go back and do it now.

- To have an achievable vision of financial security, you need a disciplined, rules-based approach to constructing and managing your portfolio.

    Do you have an investment policy statement and a qualified coach to guide you in this area of life?

Chapter 8

LET'S
ROCK AND ROLL!

C ongratulations! You made it to the last chapter! By reading this book, you've taken the first giant step toward making life after 50 your best years yet.

As you read these final pages, I hope you're now convinced that the coming years will be an exciting time, filled with opportunities to learn, grow, and do all the things that make life rewarding and worthwhile. I hope you agree that we rock and rollers are an innovative generation, capable of long, healthy, and fulfilling lives. Most important, I hope you've taken time to consider a compelling and exhilarating vision for your future.

Despite my optimism on this subject, a lot of media articles have called our generation an age-related disaster waiting to happen. According to them, American society won't be able to cope with millions upon millions of us doddering old souls. They portray us as a potential plague of locusts, scouring the landscape clean, leaving nothing for the generations that follow. As you've undoubtedly discovered by now, I have a completely different prediction. I believe the rock and roll generation is about to launch its next revolution, changing forever the way society views life after 50 and the way people age. Let's take a peek and see what this next revolution might bring.

Life After 50: The Best Years Yet

"I have enjoyed greatly the second blooming . . . suddenly you
find—at the age of 50, say—that a whole new life
has opened before you."
—Agatha Christie, British mystery writer

Research indicates that many rock and rollers intend to remain active and financially self-sufficient by continuing to work during the "retirement" years. In an article titled "Great Jobs" (*AARP Magazine,* Nov./Dec. 2003), writer Russell Wild reported, "Sixty-eight percent of workers between the ages of 50 and 70 plan to work in retirement or never retire, and by 2015 about 20 percent of America's workforce will be 55 or older (in 2000 it was 13 percent)." Unlike our parents' generation, few of us will leave our jobs, homes, and friends to spend the next 20 or 30 years vegetating in retirement communities. What will we do instead? Here are some possibilities.

Enjoy Our Increased Leisure Time

Ever since the Middle Ages, people have been slaves to the mechanical clock. The Industrial Age somehow conveyed the idea that leisure time was immoral. Today, we complain of 60- or 70-hour workweeks, yet we're unable to successfully integrate our work and leisure time. Instead, we oscillate between all work and all play, living unbalanced lives.

In the future, I believe we'll create a better balance between our work time and leisure time. Perhaps we'll follow the example of Wes, our friend from chapter 3. He cut back to two-thirds time by taking off Fridays, every other Thursday, and one additional day each month. Or perhaps we'll be like Bob, a 79-year-old former business owner who spends five months a year enjoying his leisure time in Indiana and the other seven months in Florida, where he works 20 to 30 hours a week. As our generation begins the move toward enjoying more leisure time, I think we'll see a number of variations on the old retirement theme. I believe we'll start hearing the term *semiretirement* more often than *retirement.*

Take Lengthy Sabbaticals to Rethink Our Lives

Taking a sabbatical during our 50s or 60s to rethink our lives may become a commonplace event. I believe many of us will "graduate" from our jobs or careers and move to our true calling in life. We may remain in a similar job role or field, but we'll focus on the areas we're most passionate about and diversify our interests.

As I interviewed people for this book, I found many who were doing exactly that. Curt, a 45-year-old entrepreneur, was a founder of a technology consulting firm. Shortly after his company went public, Curt became disillusioned with its new focus on short-term earnings and the loss of core values on which the company had been founded. He decided to take two years off to enjoy his family and rethink his life. He took classes on entrepreneurship, then started another technology consulting firm. Today he lives in a community he loves, where he happily works from his home office. Some days, he takes his wireless computer to the local Internet café and conducts business from there. He maintains an executive office for meeting with clients, and he thoroughly enjoys his reinvented life.

As increasing numbers of our generation decide to pursue similar options, I believe the marketplace will respond to our demand for courses, seminars, and other supportive materials to help us in our quest.

Reap the Benefits of Healthcare Advances

Windell, a client of mine, once told me, "I have two stents and I've had hernia surgery. If it weren't for the technology, my wife would be rolling me out to the beach in a wheelchair. Instead, I'm getting ready to start a new business."

The healthcare industry has made tremendous strides in our

lifetime, leading to substantial improvements in our quality of life and longevity. Fritz French, vice president of corporate marketing and communications for Guidant Corporation, a leading cardiovascular medical device manufacturer, offers the following example: "To go back just 20 years, people had bypass surgery when they had blockages in their arteries. Then along came balloon angioplasty in the mid '80s as a much less invasive way to open up the artery. In the '90s we had stents, little metal scaffolds that hold the artery open. In the last couple of years, we've learned to apply time-released drugs to the stents to prevent scar tissue and artery reclogging. Today, less than 10 percent of these stents clog up after they've been placed."

Recent developments have been astonishing, but new advancements on the horizon promise even more improvements in health and longevity. Mark Kershisnik, executive director of market research for Eli Lilly and Company, says, "Our parents' generation used the technology of the early 1900s to create a higher quality of life. Now, our generation is tasked with the next step: innovation. The innovation frontier has a lot to do with understanding biological processes; we've literally engineered things beyond our ability to use them. For example, we can make artificial limbs today but we don't know how to hook them up. We understand the physical engineering side and the specialty materials, but we don't understand the biological side. Our generation is tasked with the next major wave of innovation."

Kershisnik continues, "Innovation occurs as waves followed by periods of application. Innovation is the hard part because it takes enormous investment, and the return is not high. We're really paving the way for our children and their children. They may be able to have life expectancies of 120 years or more, and their quality of life could go up dramatically, because we're leaving a legacy of innovation."

Dr. David Wong, a medical advisor for Eli Lilly with a background in internal medicine, echoes Mark's emphasis on continued innovation. "Right now, because of technology, society is very demanding," he said. "They're pushing those of us who can do the research and bring about innovation to do so. They say, 'We've got this technology that can be used in computers. Why can't you use it to make a better limb or to make my kidneys function like they did when I was a young boy?' Society will be demanding, and I think we owe it to them to keep up with technology."

Enjoy Our Abundance in All Its Forms

After age 50, almost all life transitions will involve money and personal finance. It will be more important than ever to make the connection between our lives and our investments.

When it comes to finances, many people today consider the whole area an anxiety-producing topic. They're afraid they're going to get bad advice. They're worried that they'll outlive their money. As you learned in the last chapter, I believe the solution can be found in the emerging field of personal wealth management.

With personal wealth management, we'll see a functional, win-win relationship between clients and their advisors. Personal wealth managers will focus on helping people create a compelling vision of their future lives and integrating customized portfolio management and personal finance through good coaching and education. A personal wealth manager will be someone who understands and is part of the client's life, dreams, and goals.

This emerging business model that encourages a client-centered rather than a sales-centered relationship will be a major break-through for the financial services industry. Although personal wealth management is in the early, innovative stages of its S-curve, I'm confident that the rock and roll generation will demand and ultimately receive the service we deserve.

With life vision coaching as part of a personal wealth man-agement strategy, dealing with finances can be a rewarding expe-rience. When people are coached through the process by a caring, competent advisor, they can begin to develop a much more func-tional relationship between their money and their lives. With an advisor who educates clients and keeps them focused, rock and rollers are sure to make consistent progress toward their goals.

Sherrie, a 56-year-old research scientist, was eagerly awaiting her retirement. She began counting down the days a few years in advance, and even threw herself a party when she was one year away.

Sherrie and her husband decided to move to the mountains after they retired, so they bought a cozy cabin and decided to give it a trial run. After three days, Sherrie was shocked to discover how bored she felt. Unhappily, she told her husband, "Is this what it's going to be like after I retire? We're going to have to sell this place. I can't do this."

Sherrie realized she'd been so focused on moving away from her job that she hadn't given any thought to moving *toward* something new. She had no idea what that something new might be, but she knew she had to find out. Heading for the Internet, she discovered my firm's Web site and gave me a call. She liked the idea of customized investment management, but she was most intrigued by the concept of life vision coaching. She was eager to work with someone who could help her create a compelling vision for her future and show her how to use her money to fulfill that vision.

When we met to talk about their situation, I coached Sherrie and her husband through the Wealth Management Benchmark. They determined which issues were important to them, each issue's level of completeness, and when each issue would be addressed. The first issue we addressed was investor education. Sherrie, an analytical and intelligent woman, understood concepts she hadn't understood before and discovered mistakes she'd made in the past.

The second issue was life vision coaching. When Sherrie met with Craig Overmyer, our life vision coach, he helped her shift her focus from retirement to the next purposeful thing in her life. Describing their first coaching session, Craig said, "She was so terrified to think about what she would do after retirement that she was on the verge of tears. As a more compelling vision began to emerge for her, her tears of fear turned to tears of joy. Yes, maybe she would still move to the mountains, but her focus wouldn't be just cleaning the house, reading books, and walking in the woods. Instead, she envisioned herself connecting with a new community of people with whom she could be purposeful in her activities. She started viewing her new life as an opportunity to live in a safe and beautiful environment."

The burgeoning field of personal wealth management is not just about money; it's about envisioning rewarding, fulfilling life experiences and developing strategies for making them come true. I hope and predict this new model will become the norm in financial services as our innovative generation wages our longevity revolution.

Focus on Ourselves and What We Can Offer

For most people, the first 50 years were about raising a family or succeeding at a career. In our first 50 years, we paid our dues, we sacrificed, and we had more character-building experiences than most of us probably care to remember. However, we learned from our experiences, both good and bad.

After age 50, we still have responsibilities but now our lives can be more about us—our goals, dreams, desires, and aspirations. Dr. Dick Haid, an expert on mentoring adults through life transitions, describes this period as the third quarter of life. "The third quarter is 'I am myself'—you're working on relationships, learning, and spiritual development. You're not the warrior you once were. You're more caring and compassionate, your grandkids are really important. You think about your gifts and how you can give them to the world."

I hope this book inspires you to make the third quarter of your life a time of total wealth and abundance. Please use it as a tool and take advantage of the knowledge you now possess.

You've probably read other books or attended seminars, and when you were done, nothing different occurred. You might even have a binder or two from some personal-development event collecting dust on a bookshelf in your home or office. Don't let that happen to this book. Don't let it get buried away somewhere. Use it often to review the seven keys, update your vision, and monitor your progress toward your future life.

Are You Ready for the Next Revolution?

Our generation has an unprecedented opportunity, not only for ourselves as individuals but for society as a whole. In the 1960s, we witnessed a cultural revolution. Now it's time for the next revolution—one that will permanently change the way society views life after 50. Few people will take the action necessary to participate in this revolution. Will you be one of them?

If you decide to participate, you'll be among the bold pioneers blazing a trail toward healthy longevity. You'll have to be creative, develop your own strategies, and not expect a great deal of positive reinforcement. Right now, the longevity revolution is in the earliest stage of its development cycle. Not many people have bought into it yet. Very few Americans are creating a compelling vision or taking the best possible care of their health. Hardly anyone has an adequate exercise program, let alone a training mentality. Very few take advantage of educational opportunities, and even fewer take time to discover their passion or explore a second career.

Remember, if you want the same results as everyone else, just do what they do. To get different results, you'll have to think counterintuitively. People may laugh when you talk about aspiring to healthy longevity. They may scoff at you when you describe a compelling vision of your future life, just like they scoffed at the first horseless carriages. That's the price you pay for being a revolutionary, but it's worth it, because eventually others will be inspired by you and will begin to follow your lead.

Change won't happen overnight; it takes time for a vision to take root. However, the seeds have been planted and cognitive dissonance—that spontaneous drive state that occurs when beliefs and actions are not aligned—is already beginning to sprout. When I tell people, "Life after 50 can be your best years yet," or "As you get older, you can get better," they usually don't buy into it completely. But when I ask people, "Aren't you having more rewarding and fulfilling experiences today than you used to have? Aren't you having a lot more fun?" most of them say, "Yeah, I guess I am. I'm healthy and life has never been better." We've been somewhat brainwashed in our culture to believe that youth was the ultimate goal and getting older meant getting worse, but we're starting to see that it's just not true. Life after 50 can be our best years yet.

Many of the things I've discussed in this book will require a radical paradigm shift. You may have to change decades of pre-programmed thinking just to accept some of the concepts you've read about here. Ideas like visioning and healthy aging may seem completely impossible to you. If so, please consider the following.

Pretend it's 1970. You and I are talking together, and I'm making predictions about the future. We're wearing our bell-bottom jeans, and "I'll Be There" by the Jackson Five is playing on the transistor radio. Richard Nixon is president of the United States, Ronald Reagan has just been reelected governor of California, and young Arnold Schwarzenegger is the reigning Mr. Universe. How do you think you'd react if I told you that someday Nixon would be impeached, Reagan would become president, and Mr. Universe would be governor of the Golden State? Or that we'd talk to each other on miniature phones like the one Maxwell Smart carries in his shoe? Or that we'd someday be able to communicate instantaneously with people around the world using wireless computers the size of a notebook? What if I told you doctors would learn how to transplant hearts and implant artificial hips? Or that as 50-year-old grandparents, we'd act and feel like healthy 35-year-olds? It would have taken a vivid imagination and a very open mind to even consider the possibilities.

That's what I'm asking you to do today. Be willing to look

into the future and see what it might hold, even if some of the ideas seem inconceivable right now. We're truly on the verge of a longevity revolution, and this is your chance to be part of it.

Everything we think we know about life after 50 is about to explode. If you thought the countercultural revolution of the '60s was a big deal, button up your bell bottoms because the rock and roll generation is about to do it again. The last time was child's play. We were basically kids. Now we're at the top of our game. This next revolution will be led by corporate executives, professionals, entrepreneurs, and business owners. We're older, we're wiser, and we control vast amounts of wealth. We have no intention of silently slinking away into a Sun City sunset. We came into this world with a boom and we changed everything in our path, but the best is truly yet to come because it's never too late to live your dreams, and you're never too old to rock and roll!

Tom Hardin

About Thomas L. Hardin

Thomas L. Hardin, CMT, CFP, is the CEO and Chief Investment Officer of Canterbury Financial Group. As Chief Investment Officer, he oversees all portfolio management and investment activity. His career encompasses more than 28 years of investment management experience and 25 years in personal wealth management and personal financial coaching.

Tom has what may be the most diverse experience in the financial management industry today. After earning a bachelor's degree with a major in business from Skidmore College in Saratoga Springs, New York, he received his certification in portfolio management from the renowned University of Chicago Graduate School of Business. In addition, he has earned the following designations: Certified Financial Planner (CFP), Chartered Market Technician (CMT), and Chartered Retirement Planning Consultant (CRPC).

Tom lives in Zionsville, Indiana, with his wife, Kim.

ABOUT GAIL FINK

Gail Fink is a freelance writer and editor with more than 30 years of professional experience. Her writing and editing credits encompass all types of media, including books, audiotapes, newspaper and magazine columns, Web sites, e-newsletters, and online educational courses. She covers a wide variety of topics, including personal development, spirituality, business, health, nutrition, travel, medicine, and more.

Gail resides in San Diego, California, with her husband, Robert. She turns 50 this year and eagerly looks forward to her best years yet.

Recommended Reading

Exercise

Bill Hartman, PT
www.prperformance.com
Top-rated site for golf fitness training, including flexibility, strength, and power.

Clarence Bass' Ripped Enterprises
www.cbass.com
At age 65, Bass has the physique of someone half his age. His site offers many of his health and fitness-related books and products.

JP Fitness, Little Rock, Arkansas
www.jeanpaul.com
This site has one of the best fitness discussion forums on the Internet, with participants ranging from teens to 80 years of age.

◆　◆　◆

Strength Training Past 50 by Wayne Westcott, PhD, and Thomas Baechle. Human Kinetics Publishers: 1997. Teaches the basics of a strength-training program and provides various levels of workouts, depending on capabilities.

Strong Women Stay Young by Miriam Nelson, PhD, and Sarah Weinick, PhD. Bantam: 2000. Updated scientific information about muscle, bone, and balance; includes exercises and a new men's chapter.

Weight Training Fundamentals by David Sandler. Human Kinetics Publishers: 2003. Teaches the basics of a strength training program.

Finance and Investing

Effort-Less Marketing for Financial Advisors by Steve Moeller. American Business Visions: 1999. Five steps to a super-profitable business and a wonderful life.

Investment Psychology Explained by Martin J. Pring. John Wiley & Sons: 1993. This book delivers a renewed appreciation of the classic trading principles that have worked time and time again.

Health and Longevity

2 Young 2 Retire
www.2young2retire.com
This site offers ideas, stories, and links to businesses and organizations that can help you redefine life in the later years.

Alliance for Aging Research
www.agingresearch.org
Search for health info by topic, read the latest research, and take the Living to 100 quiz.

Healthy Living with Teresa Tanoos
www.healthylivinginfo.com
The Healthy Living TV and radio shows, magazine, and Web site were designed to educate the general public with consumer-friendly health information and medical news in an easy-to-understand format.

RealAge
www.realage.com
RealAge provides unique personal health management tools that educate, empower, and motivate healthy behavior. The RealAge test compares biological to chronological age.

◆ ◆ ◆

8 Weeks to Optimum Health by Andrew Weil, MD. Ballantine Books: 1998. Weil combines the best of traditional and complementary medicine to provide a holistic approach to health.

Ageless Body, Timeless Mind by Deepak Chopra, MD. Harmony: 1998 (reissue edition). Chopra's best-selling formula for making your biological clock stand still.

Anatomy of an Illness by Norman Cousins. Bantam: 1991 (reissue edition). The classic account of the late Norman Cousins, who mobilized his body's resources and used his mind as an effective weapon in his battle against a crippling disease.

Nutrition

American Dietetic Association
www.eatright.org
Find a dietitian in your area; general nutritional information; recommended books.

Center for Nutrition Policy and Promotion of the USDA
www.usda.gov/cnpp
Details on dietary guidelines for Americans; links to other sites.

Food and Nutrition Information Center (FNIC) of the U.S. Department of Agriculture (USDA)
www.nal.usda.gov/fnic/consumersite
Information about food and nutrition topics most frequently asked about by the public, such as FDA regulation of dietary supplements and dietary guidelines.

Mayo Foundation for Medical Education and Research
www.mayoclinic.com
Consumer-oriented medical information on dietary supplements, diseases, etc.

Tufts University
http://navigator.tufts.edu
Objective ratings of nutrition-related Web sites.

UC Berkeley Wellness Center
http://www.berkeleywellness.com
UC Berkeley's newsletter of nutrition, fitness, and self-care.

❖ ❖ ❖

The Essential Guide to Vitamins and Minerals (2nd ed.) by Elizabeth Somer. HarperCollins: 1996. Properties, dosages, and effects of 40 vitamins and minerals; guidelines for a vitamin-mineral–rich diet.

Strong Women Eat Well by Miriam Nelson, PhD. Perigee: 2002. Everything women need to know to make the best decisions about eating.

Super Nutrition After 50 by Denise Webb, PhD, and Elizabeth Ward, MSRD. International Ltd.: 1999. Information about age-related body changes and nutritional needs, herbs, hormone replacement therapy, and phytonutrients.

Tyler's Herbs of Choice: The Therapeutic Use of Phytomedicinals (2nd ed.) by James E. Robbers and Varro E. Tyler. Haworth Press: 1999. Descriptions of herbs, how they work, their therapeutic uses, and precautions.

Tyler's Tips: The Shopper's Guide for Herbal Remedies by George H. Constantine. Haworth Press: 2000. Easy-to-use descriptions of commercially available herbal products, their uses, benefits, origins, precautions, dosage forms, and price ranges; based on the works of Dr. Varro E. Tyler.

Personal Development

The Art of Possibility by Rosamund Stone Zander and Benjamin Zander. Penguin: 2002. Breakthrough practices for creativity and possibilities for visioning.

Excuse Me, Your Life Is Waiting by Lynn Grabhorn. Hampton Roads: 2003. Discover the astonishing power of feelings as a crucial part of visioning.

Focal Point by Brian Tracy. AMACOM: 2002. A proven system for simplifying your life, doubling your productivity, and achieving all your goals.

Near to My Heart: An American Dream by William K. Nasser, MD. Nasco Publishing: 2003. The inspiring autobiography of a respected cardiologist and entrepreneur whose life has been a series of dramatic adventures.

The Path of Least Resistance by Robert Fritz. Ballantine: 1989. Learn how to be a creative force in your own life, and how to get more done with less effort.

RealTime Coaching™ by Ron Ernst. Leadership Horizons: 2001. This book is for leaders, managers, and supervisors serious about getting the job done with and through their employees. Increase productivity, improve profitability, reduce turnover, and enhance customer service by building a new foundation based on self-responsibility and self-accountability.

Success Is a Decision of the Mind by Paul Wilson and Dr. Craig Overmyer. Insight: 2004. With B.I.O. (Business Inside Out), the ultimate business decision, the true leader in any organization can be found within each person. Also includes the 7 Response-abilities of Wealth-Health Investment.

◆ ◆ ◆

RESOURCES

Canterbury Financial Group

Canterbury Financial Group is an independently owned, fee-only, Registered Investment Advisor listed with the Securities and Exchange Commission. We're committed to helping our clients create prosperity, both financially and in their quality of life. We believe win-win relationships are the only kind our clients deserve—and the only kind we're willing to have.

At Canterbury, we specialize in a new process called personal wealth management: We help successful individuals achieve *total wealth and abundance* in all their forms. For more information about personal wealth management, or to schedule a personal interview, please feel free to contact us.

Toll-free: 800.340.0234 (800.3400.CFG)
info@canterburygroup.com
www.canterburygroup.com

Dr. Craig Overmyer

Dr. Craig Overmyer is a contributing author in two books, *Dynamic Health* and *Success Is a Decision of the Mind,* and a professional member of the National Speakers Association. He appears regularly on the TV program and in the magazine published by *Healthy Living with Teresa Tanoos.* Craig provides keynote speaking, training, and coaching for Fortune 500 companies. His online, teleconference, and live training programs include:

- **RealTime Coaching**™ for managers and supervisors to create great work groups

- **Vital Decisions** for bringing out followership in leaders, and leadership in followers among senior executives, managers, and employees of organizations

- **Heal*thy* Living Coaching** for improved patient commitment and compliance for their own healthcare vision

Information about Craig's training programs, e-books, and other products is available. In addition, meeting planners can find out more about booking Dr. Craig Overmyer at the following Web sites:

www.canterburyspeaks.com
www.bio-asap.com
Toll-free: 800.340.0234